The Cool Girl's Guide to Knitting

Nicki Trench

The Cool Girl's Guide to Knitting

Nicki Trench

Everything the novice knitter needs to know

p

This is a Parragon Publishing Book
First published in 2005

Parragon Publishing
Queen Street House
4 Queen Street
Bath BA1 1HE, UK

ISBN 1-40545-232-3

The author would like to thank the following people without whom the book would have beven a lot less fun to write:
Debra Cox, Rob & Caroline Cowan, Adam Hawes, John Lockwood, Dee Maher, Maddy Perkins, Roger Perkins, Zara Poole,
Gabriela Sindelova, Vicki Wanless.
Knitwear Designers: Vikki Haffenden, Jane Rota, Nicki Trench
Models: Angus, Camilla Perkins, Tom Sheffield, Roxy Walton
Stylist: Vikki Haffenden
Assistant Stylist: Hannah Jenkinson
Also thanks to: The Revolver Vodka Bar and Boogaloo, Hastings, England. "Knitters from here" at the here shop, Bristol, England.

For Butler and Tanner:
Project Editor: Julian Flanders
Editor: Emma Clegg
Designer: Carole McDonald

Location and techniques photography: Carole McDonald
Studio photography: Don Last
Art works: Sue Lee

Additional photos provided by Corbis UK page 8,
Debbie Bliss pages 10 & 11, Getty Images page 7,
Rex Features page 11, Rowan Yarns pages 2, 10 & 11

Printed in Malaysia

Contents

PART ONE

Knit then...

... and now

Why Has Knitting Come Back Into Fashion?

The simple answer is that such an addictive pastime can't just disappear without making a comeback. Knitting is given a new lease of life as it is rediscovered by each new generation. Recently knitting's stock has soared because modern couturiers have for several seasons presented beautifully designed knitwear with a hefty price tag and it's not hard to see that these same designs can be made at home for a fraction of the price. And, besides, what other activity can turn the making of something into a party?

Ancient purls of wisdom

Knitters rule – and there is no doubt about it. Was there a time when we didn't knit? Well, there must have been. The earliest traces of knitting as we know it are cotton socks and other knitted fragments dating from AD 1200–1500 in Islamic Egypt, although anklet socks with a stocking-stitch-type construction have also been found in Egypt dating from as early as the third century. So there's an important lesson: if your civilization is in final decline, always keep your feet warm.

The Britons kept sheep and wove wool long before the Roman invasion, and the establishment by the Romans of a factory at Winchester, England improved their methods. Knitting came into the European picture in the 5th century, when the Moors from North Africa invaded Spain.

By the 13th century England was the greatest wool-producing country in Europe. Knitting was the principal method of making socks and women's stockings. Hosiery, the name still used to describe these products, is derived from the old English word "hose", which means "a covering for the leg". Gradually knitting came to be used to make more elaborate garments such as sweaters and jackets and other items of fitted clothing. Although this does depend on your definition of "elaborate" – if you've ever turned a heel on a sock you'll know that this is no rudimentary process.

The image of women knitting "while the guillotine falls" during the French Revolution is striking, but it owes more to Charles Dickens's novel A Tale of Two Cities than it does to any historical fact.

Knitting wasn't always considered the occupation of women. Indeed, some historians think that men invented the craft, probably fishermen developing a technique for making fishing nets. The knitted craft remains closely allied with the fishing trade, with fishermen still wearing Ganseys, or traditional fishermens' sweaters, so densely knitted in worsted yarn that they are almost windproof and waterproof. Individual knitted designs were often used for the various fishing village communities. In the marshy Les Landes area in southwest France, the medieval peasants kept huge flocks of sheep. The shepherds would walk around on stilts so that they could take longer steps, cover more ground and see further. They used to knit while they walked using a knitting belt to keep their wool safe. They were vegetarian and used the sheep for their manure rather than meat, so they didn't kill them. They knitted their own gaiters to keep their feet warm and felted their own jackets from the fleeces of their sheep.

Women do their bit for the war effort knitting socks from recycled wool circa 1940.

Knitting for victory

In the 20th century women were urged to knit for the troops in the two world wars, especially World War One when the men faced severe shortages of socks, undershirts, and washcloths. In this conflict, the image of the resolute soldier shivering in a trench was implanted in the minds of the world's womenfolk. In the 1939–45 war, millions of knitted pieces were produced. Posters produced by organizations such as the American Red Cross in 1943 urged womenfolk to keep knitting: "Our boys need SOX, knit your bit". It was a real act of love, and even the British boys of the Eighth Army, sweltering in the Western Desert, could not help but be moved upon receipt of a lovingly hand-knitted item from home. There was even a free Red Cross kit featuring the hand-dyed yarn, a pattern and the double-pointed and finishing needles necessary to make a pair of military socks. During this period, knitting was even being featured on the front of *Life* magazine.

Fashion revolution

In the 1950s and 1960s, color in knitting arrived with a bang. After the drabness of the war, color and motif knitting became the new knitting fads. Girls were taught to knit in schools, where it was still regarded as a necessity and a useful skill. The knitted "twin-set" comprising a cardigan over a matching short-sleeved top, came into fashion. It made another brief comeback in the 1970s and will almost inevitably surface again in future decades.

Did knitting ever really go away?

Frankly, yes. The 1970s and 1980s were a particularly brutal time for knitting. Girls, not wanting to look like their grandmas, turned their backs on knitting and immersed themselves in glam rock. The increased availability of low-cost machine-knitted items made knitting an expensive luxury, when you could buy a sweater off the peg cheaper than it could be knitted. It was the start of the convenience culture, with equivalent cultural parallels being sheetrock, fish sticks, and instant mashed potato.

There was an abundance of cheap clothing made in artificial fibers, with the novelty of chucking everything in

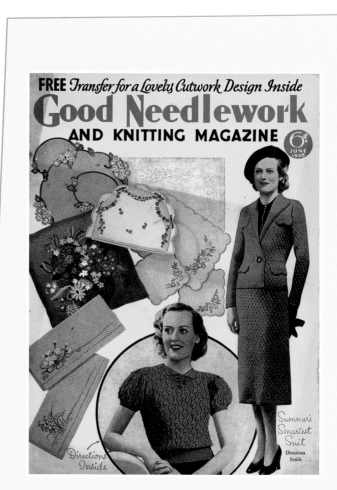

During the 1940s and 1950s knitting was tasteful and high fashion…

The Cool Girl's Guide to Knitting

the washing machine being much too hard to resist. Wool started to be replaced by acrylic yarn. As wool shops were interested only in selling manmade fibers, the pure natural brands were pushed aside to make way for the vibrant colors and wacky styles of the era. Rather than being appreciated for its beauty, wool was instead associated with heavy and itchy knits. And with a washing machine in every kitchen, who was going to mess around with that woollen material that shrank and clumped up as soon as it went anywhere near water?

The craft industry in general went into decline as women rose to the challenge of being equal players in the workplace. Women either embraced capitalism and adopted big hair and big shoulders, or put on a boiler suit and picketed bus stations as part of the feminist "Reclaim the Night" campaign. Knitting was what you didn't do – it had become a symbol of passivity and staying at home. Whether you dressed to the political left or right, staying in just wasn't an option.

Knitting was no longer being taught in schools and was slowly being relegated to the confines of "hippy" culture, in a time before hippy was hip. Knitters began to develop a reputation for being part of the macrobiotic, faddy set and nobody with a Filofax would be caught dead with knitting needles or a crochet hook at this time.

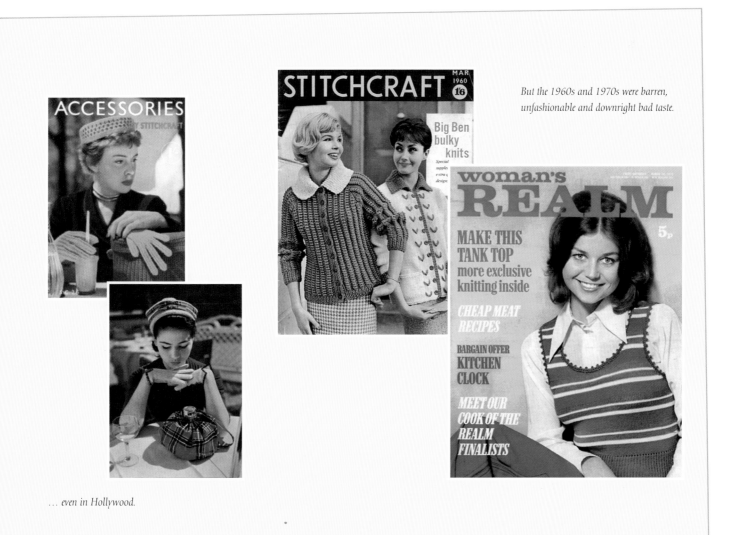

But the 1960s and 1970s were barren, unfashionable and downright bad taste.

… even in Hollywood.

Knitting Bites Back

Knitting is now making a comeback and defying the idea that it cannot form an enriching part of a modern woman's life. Women now realize that they can juggle different aspects of themselves, so can, if they choose, be mothers and craftswomen, have serious careers and still go clubbing on a Saturday night. The knitting industry has been quick to recognize this. In an effort to modernize the reputation of knitting, companies such as Vogue and Rowan have produced knitting pattern books rather than leaflets, and their quality photography now shows knitting to be at the height of fashion, bearing no resemblance to the old images of dull men in balaclavas and grimacing children sporting itchy swimwear. Of course, you can also buy high-quality knitwear, but when the idea of an acquired skill comes into play, the cost ceases to be the point.

As well as stylish patterns, the yarn itself has taken on a new life. The old acrylic fibers used to build you up with static electricity, but now top-quality, natural wools are mixed with a small amount of manmade fibers, restoring the tradition of natural wools while at the same time benefiting from modern-day developments. The easy-care results are another bonus that has drawn people back to knitting.

The cult of the accessory

The TV schedule is full of home-improvement programs and knitting has also moved in this direction, becoming a source of home-decoration ideas and accessories. Instead of knitting only sweaters and complicated cardigans, knitters can now bring individuality and creativeness into their home by making items such as cushion covers and throws. You're not just knitting now – you're following a lifestyle pattern.

Yarn producers have tried to encourage knitters back to the craft by producing specialty yarn. The sumptuous mixes of yarn, such as Merino wool, Cashmere, and Alpaca, are hard to resist. The colors have also been brought up to date with historical heritage palettes that tone in with the specialty paints in our modern interiors. All the perceived advantages of using pure manmade fibers have therefore vanished. People are knitting with fabrics other than wool: there is ribbon yarn, chenille, eyelash yarn, and hand-dyed slubs, along with the superchunky yarn that knits up on giant-size needles, meaning that knitting is no longer a time-intensive pastime. If weather forecasts predict snow tomorrow, you can whip up several superchunky hats in a single evening.

21st-century knitting

Knitwear is in fashion – just pick up a copy of any fashion magazine and you will see hand-knitted scarves, sweaters and skirts in the new textures and superchunky styles.

As a result, further-education textile courses have a new influx of students enrolling for knitting. The knitters of today regard what they do as a branch of art and in their minds they are a world away from the familiar image of grandma knitting for her grandchildren. There is no need, however, to ignore those knitters who've kept the craft alive through the years; grandmas are now hailed as new gurus by the young knitters of today.

Celebrity knitting – the new yoga

There are often articles in the local and national press with a knitting story. Knitting seems now to have caught the eye of the media, particularly when a hot celebrity gets out his or her needles. Knitting is now hailed as the "new yoga" as celebrities, young professionals and yarn enthusiasts from all walks of life are getting down to knitting. Geri Halliwell, Julia Roberts, Catherine Zeta-Jones, Russell Crowe, Kate Moss, Sarah Jessica Parker, Daryl Hannah, Uma Thurman, Julianne Moore, Courtney Cox-Arquette, and Madonna are all knitting on and off set – it's obviously an ideal pastime between takes and the passion of these stars is influencing the proliferation of new knitters all over the world.

Psychological warmth

And is it any wonder? Knitting is a wonderful retreat from an increasingly tough world. It's calming, primeval, just like dancing to a plain drumbeat – in, round, through and off. The soft touch of the yarn is comforting, a pleasant contrast to the harshness of the computer keyboard and our new culture of tough words such as hard drive, megabyte, metatag and USB. The restorative powers of knitting demonstrates the calming effect of repetition. As you knit,

your breathing adjusts to its rhythm and the whole process becomes a soothing and meditative experience.

The effect on your mind is similar to distance running or saying a rosary – it puts you within reach of a higher awareness. Your mind begins to behave in the same way as your brain works just before you go to sleep – relaxed, but at the same time aware – and enters what is called "a suggestible state". If you put on language learning tapes while you're knitting, you'll be truly amazed at your progress. Or try listening to baroque music as you knit – Bach, Vivaldi, Corelli, and Pachabel are all big hitters in the world of baroque 'n' roll. Bach, especially, gives you a day ticket to nirvana.

Socks and the City: Sarah Jessica Parker and Kristin Davis chatting, smiling, and, of course, knitting on set, winter 2001.

There's a real zen to knitting – and it makes you realize that the zen is in the task itself. On a recent knit night, as the stitch count grew higher, I began a conversation with the woman next to me. We were so intent on the job in hand that we didn't make eye contact, normally regarded as essential for effective communication, during the whole conversation. No, on we went talking about real issues and exchanging considered views. It felt comforting at the time, however astonishing in retrospect.

Rock 'n' roll or knit 'n' purl?

But the real hardcore of knitters are being hailed as guerrilla knitters. They have taken up the craft as a new cause, promoting knitting as a hip and cool hobby that should be taken very seriously. One such group is Cast Off, formed in 2000 and based in London, England. Its members' aims are to encourage the art of knitting and urge people to pick up their needles wherever they are – in bars, nightclubs, or on the subway. They have organized knit-in parties on the Circle Line of the London Underground where knitters pop on at their stop in a chosen carriage, knit away for a few circles around London and get off when they've finished. Cast Off has also organized a knitting event at London's Victoria & Albert Museum that an amazing 4,000 people attended. The atmosphere was steamy with participants knitting and purling to the rhythms of rock. There was a DJ, beer, and someone in a pink knitted Elvis wig, people were dancing with their knitting, and everyone who came in was offered free needles and yarn. More amazing still, there was an even mix of women and men – this was definitely not knitting as our grandmothers knew it. Cast Off also holds "knit-ins" at summer festivals. There are other similar groups emerging around the UK.

Inspired by the book *Stitch 'n Bitch* by Debbie Stoller, Stitch 'n' Bitch groups have really taken off. There are knitting-group meetings in every state, with people from all walks of life getting together at cafés, bars and community centers to work on projects, help each other with their knitting projects and chat. According to the Craft Yarn Council of America, the number of knitters under 35 grew by more than 400 per cent between 1998 and 2000.

It seems that knitting circles in the USA are following the example set by book clubs in providing fun, companionship, and community. There is a big knitting community at Yale, where there is a whole scene of women very serious about their handiwork; one student even knitted her way through her math classes one semester and later married her math teacher. A couple of male students turned up at the Yale Stitch 'n' Bitch classes, only to be turned away for very obviously being attracted to the classes for the girls not the needles. Men interested in knitting, however, are warmly welcomed.

The internet has undoubtedly had a huge influence on the rise of knitters in the 21st century. The buying of knitting products has soared with the emergence of websites selling yarn and patterns via mail order, while knitting–forum chat rooms help knitters keep in touch and bring together the knitting community. So knitting has now emerged well and truly as a cool hobby – increasing numbers of people are discovering that the rhythmic clacking of the needles and comforting feel of the yarn let the demands of 21st-century pressures slip away and off the needle.

Extreme Knitting

Knitters are getting so obsessed with their knitting that they can't put it down. So forget extreme ironing and take up extreme knitting.

Knitting Groups

They say that staying in is the new going out, and what is better than staying in with friends doing something you enjoy? And a few casual drinks aren't going to be a cause of stress. It might mean you lose a few stitches, but nobody is going to breathalyse you while knitting under the influence.

Why knitting groups?

Knit groups started when women used to knit for extra money in the evenings. They would go to each other's houses to save on candles and heat and, without doubt, to chat. Nothing beats hanging out with like-minded people who have a shared intent. Men watch football and talk about sport whereas women knit and talk about life, the universe, and everything. If you have the choice between joining a knitting night or a book club, which would you choose? Sure, the book club is a great idea and it means you'll have a real intellectual challenge, but it's still consuming rather than producing, and you may find that really great books are ignored by the club in favor of the works of a no-hope literary-prize wannabe.

Knitting is productive, cheap and safe, but most of all it is therapeutic. As our society becomes increasingly impersonal, a group that provides mutual support and fun, is cheaper than many other evening activities, and offers more effective results is very appealing. Once you start knitting you'll find that you start communicating with your fellow knitters, sometimes pouring out your emotions and you can end up disclosing all your secrets. Knitting is also an excellent way of giving up smoking, as your hands are kept busy and, in any case, you might set fire to your yarn. It's cheaper than psychotherapy and who wants to sit on a couch with nothing to do?

Professional women find themselves thrust into a tough and competitive male world and this can take its toll. Knitting is an ideal opportunity to get out of the get up and go drive, switch off and do the girly bonding thing, offering a chill-out for women who are frantically trying to do it all. Knitting tends to appeal to creative people and women who are not afraid of being girly. "Knit night" groups are being organized in public knitting venues as well as private houses. A screening of *Bridget Jones's Diary* took place in London, England exclusively for a London-based knitting group. Groups of knitters are sprouting up everywhere in the UK, the USA, and Europe. Meetings are being held for relaxation and for the pursuit of art. While some women choose to adopt feminism, social climbing, and sexual equality, others adopt creative crafts.

For whatever reason, most just like to meet for fun, to drink coffee, hot chocolate or wine, and eat cake. Most knitters are female, but there are a growing number of men joining the knitting groups. The members are principally in their 20s and 30s, but they are also drawn from a wide range of ages. The cult is so established that there are now knitting and surfing holidays being organized on the coast and you can even, if you choose, combine knitting and parachuting.

Knitting promotes communication and helps produce a positive and productive attitude to life.

Knitting and Dating

Follow these rules and your purls may get you a diamond

RULE 1

Do not knit your boyfriend a sweater until you are well and truly into your relationship (at least 10 years).

There is a well-known superstition that if you knit your boyfriend a sweater you will, within a week, be on your own. Much of the abandoned, unfinished knitting in the attic can be attributed to lost boyfriends. If you start knitting him a sweater, it is probably only at the point of shaping the left-hand shoulder that he leaves you for the blonde up the road.

RULE 2

Do not wear itchy fabrics on your first date.

Instead, choose something silky with a satin feel. Snuggle up in something cashmere or silk – mohair or eyelash yarn might get up his nose and he may think he has an allergy to you.

RULE 3

Don't take your knitting on your first date.

As difficult as it is to put down or finish that row, leave it at home. Guys will want to feel that the attention is on them, not on your knitting.

RULE 4

Do take your knitting on your first date.

This applies only if it's a speed-dating event – this is a great opportunity to knit because if the guy you're talking to is boring, at least you can make use of the time. And if you can't find anything interesting to say, you can talk about what you're knitting.

RULE 5

Don't let dating interfere with your knitting.

Get on his good side by suggesting you both stay in and watch the football. He'll be amazed and think he's hit the jackpot – a girl who likes football! Just snuggle up next to him and whip out your knitting while he's cheering on his favorite team. Bingo, you're both happy.

RULE 6

Invest in a hands-free telephone headset.

Then you can carry on knitting when he calls you on the phone. This also helps eliminate all the "you hang up, no, you hang up" banter.

RULE 7

Make sure your needles are safely stowed away before those tender sofa moments.

You could be just at that critical moment and your #11 needles may give him a nasty surprise.

> " *Knit your hearts out with unslipping knot* "

William Shakespeare, Anthony and Cleopatra

What do we do in a knitting group?

Well, we knit and we talk… mmmmm… that's just about it. Communicating is one thing that women have a natural facility for. We support our friends, share knowledge, and help each other. Fellow knitters are reassuring and supportive of each other's knitting and there is rarely any competitive element. We discuss current affairs, problems, health, family, and work; we giggle and laugh; and sometimes we just sit in silence with the sound of our needles busying away. Silent pauses are respected, someone may be counting their stitches.

Setting up a knitting group

All you need is some knitting and a good supply of soft drinks and wine for those knitting less complicated items who don't need to keep a crystal-clear head. Once you're brave enough to tell people that you're setting up a knitting group, you'll be surprised at the number of people who will remember their half-finished knitting in the attic. They'll say it in an embarrassed and shifty way at first and then the passion will pour out with descriptions of the texture and color of the yarn as it slips through their fingers and slides off the needles. The touch and feel of the cold aluminum or the warm bamboo needles will entice such alerted minds… and then you'll find they'll be begging to come.

Monday nights are best. You're rarely hampered by other commitments and you can catch up on any gossip after the weekend in a relaxed, unthreatening atmosphere – 7.30 p.m. to 10.00 p.m. is perfect, allowing you to get home at a reasonable time. You can alternate between friends' houses. Or if you have a really comfortable venue such as a friendly bar with a supportive manager, that's perfect. But pick your bar carefully; one knitting group was recently chucked out of a bar on a Monday night. Make sure you buy a few gin and tonics during the evening and don't stand in front of the TV when the football's on. Remember, you need comfy sofas and chairs and a clean floor for your wool when it rolls out of your bag.

When people see you knitting in public, they can't resist coming over and talking to you about what you're making, especially if you're using the new funky yarn that is now so popular.

Bristol knitting group

PART TWO

What you need...

... and what to do with it

Yarn

> New types of yarns are partly responsible for knitting making such a comeback. Some are so beautiful that you just want to have that sumptuous ball of wool next to you on the sofa without a knitting needle in sight.

There are so many variations of yarn you can buy, in so many different textures and colors, that it's hard to know where to start. If you start from a pattern, then use the pattern to focus your choice of yarn and any other choices that need to be made. Or you might first discover a yarn that you just can't resist and choose a pattern afterwards.

WHERE TO BUY YARN

Department stores

These are generally a good source of yarn, although their supplies can be limited.

High-street wool stores

These more traditional specialist stores are now quite few and far between. This is generally because of a lack of demand for the often uninspiring types of yarn they used to sell. However, new specialist stores are now slowly emerging that are catering for the modern taste for natural and varied yarn.

Internet companies

The internet is probably going to be your best starting point. Internet companies have been quick to meet the growing demand for knitting yarn so you can now browse your laptop in comfort and have the yarn delivered right to your door. And what a pleasure when you receive your parcel full of knitting goodies – it's just like receiving a present in the post! Find an internet company that is willing to give you advice, too. The local wool store used to provide guidance on patterns, yarn and knitting equipment and any internet company selling yarn should fulfil the same role for you.

Charity stores

Stop at any charity store to have a look around as they can sometimes prove a good source of yarn. Obviously, there are no guarantees, but if you rummage around enough you may find something really marvelous. Remember that it will be even more important to knit a tension square if there are no labels on the yarn.

eBay

This auction site has a selection of yarn for web auction. While you can't always find an exact yarn or quantity, it's a good place for finding discount yarn.

YARN TYPES

Here is a list of yarn types that will help you unravel the vocabulary of knitting.

Wool

Wool comes from many different types of sheep, some with much softer wool than others. The fleece from the Spanish-bred Merino sheep has become popular in recent years – it's very fine and soft and available from most manufacturers. Other fine wools include Delaine Merino, Shetland, and Debouillet. Apparently there is a fine wool that comes from the North Ronaldsay sheep, which lives wild on this Orkney island in Scotland and grazes not on grass but on seaweed – and it is this that makes its underbelly fleece incredibly soft. The wool is hard to source, and it can take several days to reach the island depending on the weather. Medium wools include Dorset, Suffolk, Shropshire, and Navajo Churro; long wools include Lincoln, Cotswold, Teeswater, and Shetland; and coarse wools include Swaledale, Black Welsh Mountain,

and Cheviot. Some wool from Iceland and South America can be very rough and you may find bits of wood and straw tangled up in it. Not so perfect against your body, therefore, but good for chunky cardigans and those people who can stand the discomfort of a Tibetan hat.

Silk

Silk yarn is an expensive investment, but before you turn to a more economical hobby, just have a careful look at some. Silk creates a light and luxurious yarn that makes lovely summer tops or wraps when knitted. It can stretch, but it feels incredibly self-indulgent to the touch – and using silk yarn does give you great knitting caché.

Cotton

This yarn is light and absorbent. It is not as stretchy as wool, but you can buy a wool/cotton mix that works well. Because of its lightness, it is good for a knitted summer garment.

Other natural yarns

Yarns from animals other than sheep, namely the Angora goat (Mohair), the Alpaca (Alpaca), goats or rabbits (Angora) or the underbelly of a goat (Cashmere) are becoming hugely popular. They are very warm and comfortingly soft, the type of yarn that you want to pick up and hold to your face, cooing that you must knit something with it. These types of yarn sometimes come in a wool or silk mix.

Acrylic

This is easy to wash and inexpensive. It is not as warm as natural fibers, however, and the colors look less appealing. This yarn was one of the reasons why knitting went out of fashion in the 1970s and 1980s. Don't look at me, it's not my favorite. But it has some uses, and sometimes a blend of acrylic and wool fibers works well enough.

Ribbon yarn

Usually a manmade fiber (most often polyester), this yarn comes in a whole range of beautiful colors and textures. This fabric yarn is fantastic for knitting because it knits up well. If you are knitting a garment, try to find a yarn that has a bit of stretch in it.

Eyelash yarn

This fine and hairy yarn is usually made of polyester and is very soft and non-itchy, despite having the appearance of something off a dog's back. I wouldn't recommend knitting a whole sweater out of it unless you want to look like a yeti, but it's great for cuffs, collars, and accessories. It could be used to make a really funky bag or scarf (see page 76). Eyelash yarn is available in some truly wacky colors.

PLY

Knitting yarn is available in the following thicknesses, each one suitable for a different type of knitting.

4 ply

This thin yarn is used for making light garments, such as summer tops or baby clothes.

Double knitting (dk)

Still a fine wool, this is commonly used for fine garments and baby clothes.

Aran or Worsted

A versatile ply and the most common, this is about twice as thick as double knitting. Good for beginners.

Chunky

This is about twice as thick as Aran or worsted. It knits on larger needles and is good for sweater, hats, scarves and gloves.

Superchunky

This yarn is increasingly becoming the most popular and is largely responsible for the recent revival of interest in knitting. When knitted up into sweaters and scarves, it makes a real fashion statement. It is knitted on supersize needles, usually #19 or #35, so you can knit a hat or a scarf in one evening. It is perfect for knitters who have other things to do as well as knit.

Hanks, skeins and balls

Yarn is sold by weight and length. It is usually sold in 25g, 50g or 100g weights and the length varies according to the thickness and gauge of the yarn. The length and the weight should be given on the label.

In most stores yarn will come in a wound ball, but sometimes it will come in a hank or a skein. This is a big coil of yarn wrapped in a twist to save it from coming loose. Yarn hanks are what memories are made of. Nearly all yarn used to be packaged like this and my early memories of knitting are of holding up my aching arms for my grandmother so she could wind it into a ball. Either find someone to hold up their two arms for you (the preferable option) or, in the absence of a willing participant, push a couple of chairs together the distance of the size of the hanks, put the hank around the chairs and wind. I find that people love holding up their arms for ball winding. It's at times like this that you'll feel blessed to have a partner who's a keen and boastful fishing enthusiast ("It was *this* big!").

Reading a yarn label

There's a great deal of information on these labels and they are very useful, although the print is often small so a magnifying glass may be required. You will find the brand name, the yarn name and its knitting weight (for example dk or double knit). The label will also tell you what the yarn is made of and the length and weight of the yarn in the ball. There will be a diagram of the recommended knitting gauge, washing and ironing instructions and the recommended needle size. It will also have the yarn's shade number and the dye lot.

Don't throw the label away until you are absolutely sure you have finished with it. If you run out of yarn in the middle of knitting that last sleeve, you might need to find the same dye lot, so you will need the label to check the number when getting back to your yarn supplier. Yarn is dyed in batches (lots) and these dye lots can vary slightly, so it's always best to try to match them up if you can.

Equipment

Here is a list of the equipment and accessories that are either essential or useful to knitters.

NEEDLES

Well, how can you knit without them? Knitting needles come in several sizes. They have developed significantly since our foremothers' day, with the points getting pointier and the bamboo getting smoother.

I've seen people use knitting needles for all sorts of activities: testing to see if a cake is cooked, scratching backs, mini javelin (soon to be an Olympic sport), drumming, picking teeth and playing Ker-Plunk! My mother was even stabbed in the leg by one and still proudly shows her scar:

apparently there's nothing like a scrap in a local bingo parlor to bring out the swordswoman in us all.

Needle measurements

Just to confuse you, there are three measurements used in knitting patterns: UK, US, and metric. To confuse you even more, in the UK they no longer use the UK measurement, but the metric measurement.

Needle width

The gray needles in the thinner sizes are generally made from aluminum; as they get thicker they are made from plastic. Needle width, or the diameter of the needle, is crucial. Thick needles are usually used with thick yarn and thin needles with thin yarn. All good patterns and yarn labels will give the recommended needle size for the yarn and pattern. But, depending on the tension you wish to create in the piece, you may end up knitting with a needle size that's bigger or smaller than recommended.

Bamboo needles are becoming very popular – they have a warm feel and are more natural. It's worth investing in good-quality bamboo, as the cheaper versions tend to snag the yarn and split.

If you scour charity stores you can find all sorts of yummy needles. The needle measurement may be in old sizes, so make sure you check with a needle conversion table. I've recently seen tortoiseshell needles for sale on eBay and I've known glass needles to have been found at a charity store, so keep your eyes peeled. Remember, however, that new needles have a much pointier design and are therefore easier to knit with.

Circular needles

Circular needles have two pointy ends, shorter than normal straight needles, and a plastic length in the middle of varying sizes. They are usually used to knit in the round, particularly items such as socks or hats. Many knitters, however, also use them to knit flat work. If you are knitting something that takes lots of stitches, such as a throw, a circular needle is excellent. Make sure you choose the right length circular needle, one with a long enough centerpiece to hold the stitches. Knitters are increasingly taking to circular needles as they are so portable. They have been highly recommended in the USA as the perfect needles to take to music festivals; the short needles don't poke too far out of your bag and the knitting and needle is in one piece so you are less likely to lose your needles and ruin any valuable knitting time while away from home.

Double-pointed needles

These are just what they say – they have a point at either end of the needle. They are shorter than standard needles and usually come in packs of four or five. They are often used for knitting socks. This process is not as intimidating as it looks –

just keep knitting until you get to the next needle point. As you work you are prompted by the needles and the working sequence becomes obvious.

Cable needles

Cable needles are used to hold your stitches with knitting cables. They usually come in either large or small sizes.

TAPE MEASURE

Use a cloth tape rather than the inflexible metal ones you get in a toolbox – otherwise you might end up knitting a girder. In the old days there was always a measurement drawn on the side of patterns, but as most patterns are in magazines or books now, you need to carry your own.

SCISSORS

The cry heard most often at knit nights after "Where did you put that other bottle of wine?" is "Who's got the scissors?" It's always best to carry your own and I would suggest tying them to your knitting bag so that nobody can steal them. Medium-sized sharp ones are the best.

STITCH HOLDERS

These come in handy for holding stitches that you're not using. The safety-pin type works best, or use safety pins if you only have to hold a small number of stitches.

SEWING-UP NEEDLE

Buy a good yarn sewing-up needle with a big enough eye for the yarn you are using.

PINS

Straight pins with colored ends are used for blocking and checking tension. Ordinary straight pins will get lost in the yarn.

ROW COUNTERS

These help you record your progress by turning the counter to the number required when counting rows. This means that if you have to leave your knitting and get up for any reason you will know exactly which row you are on and can continue on your return. You are supposed to slide them to the bottom of your needle, but sometimes this feels uncomfortable when knitting with smaller needles as the counters can be a bit heavy. Try threading the row counter with a thick piece of yarn and wearing it as a necklace. It could catch on as a fashion statement and shows you are part of the knitting movement.

CROCHET HOOKS

Like knitting needles, crochet hooks come in different sizes. They are shorter than knitting needles and have a hook on one end. They are useful tools for of picking up the inevitable lost stitch or two.

NEEDLE PROTECTORS

These stop the stitches from falling off. Buy plenty of them – they're essential.

BUTTONS

Buttons can be a fabulous decoration and finish off your knitted piece to perfection. However, choose wisely. A cheap, unattractive button can undermine the quality of your garment. Make sure you choose the right size button for the buttonhole instructions in the pattern.

Buttons are made in all shapes and sizes and from many different materials: ceramic, glass, plastic, shell, metal, horn, and wood. Check the washing instructions for the buttons, as unprotected metal ones may rust.

Buttons can be used to embellish bags, hats, and cushions.

Carrying and Storing Your Knitting

MAMA'S GOT A BRAND-NEW BAG

After you've been knitting a while, you may notice the whole house being taken over by end-bits of yarn: pieces that you can't bear to throw out because "they might just come in useful one day". So you'll need to find somewhere to store them.

Baskets are good, as they show off your wool and, if well placed, make them a design feature in an interior. If you don't want to show them off, plastic stackable boxes are another storage option. Click the lid tight if you're putting them in the cellar or a loft, as mice have been known to make comfy little nests in these wool havens. And besides, who wants to see a rat wearing the same cardigan as you? Moths can also attack yarn, so if you plan on leaving the yarn unattended for a long time, investment in a few mothballs may be wise.

What should you use to carry your knitting around? About the need to do this there is no question – you must take it out and show it off, in fact, treat it like a new boyfriend. You'll surely get more interest in the knitting than the boyfriend (except any Johnny Depp look-alikes, of course). For this you will need something deep enough to keep the needles from poking out and causing injury. So you need enough room in that bag to carry bits of your knitting equipment, it needs to complement your knitting and, naturally, it should be a very hip bag. Baskets work well, but don't get one that will snag the knitting; do check that the handles are strong enough. Another idea is to make your own – the bag on page 90 is perfect and simple to make.

And don't forget – you must make a point of knitting in public. So, rock on knitting… keep the revolution alive.

Knitting Techniques

Holding your needles

Hold your needles in a cross position with the right needle behind the left. With your left hand, support both the needles with the left index finger at the back supporting the right needle and the left thumb pinching the left needle against the right one. In this way your right hand is free to work the yarn.

Having cast on (see page 26), hold the cast-on stitches on the left-hand needle. Hold the right-hand needle as you would a pen, but tilt it back slightly. Put the right-hand needle into the stitch, making sure the needles cross with the right needle behind the left. Put your left thumb on the left needle and your left index finger behind the cross so you are supporting the cross with a pinch action. Your right hand should now be free to pick up the yarn. Your left thumb should be resting about 1in (2.5cm) from the tip of the needle.

Another holding method that some people find more comfortable involves holding the right needle in the same manner as the left, not as a pen but more like a dinner knife.

If you are holding long needles, tuck the right needle under your arm to keep it from flapping about. This is how my grandmother taught me to knit. It's certainly a useful tip if the man next to you on the train is reading a paper. Although tapping a paper rhythmically with your needles as you knit makes a wonderful sound – try it.

Holding your yarn

There is a trick to holding your yarn so that your tension isn't too tight or too loose. It seems that no two knitters hold their yarn in the same way. The method that I recommend is as follows:

Pick up the yarn with your right little finger, with your palm facing upwards so the yarn end joined to the ball is caught between your little finger and third finger. Turn your hand round towards you, twisting the yarn around your little finger (1).

Now, with your palm facing down, catch the yarn with your slightly pointed index finger, keeping the yarn held by bending your last three fingers inwards. Now hold the left needle (2).

This method keeps the yarn in place so you don't have to keep picking it up or dropping the needles for every stitch. Remember to hold the needles crossed and with a pinch from the left hand.

Casting on

The best way to learn to cast on is to be taught first hand. Lure a grandma in from the street with the promise of coffee, offer to bake them a cake for a good cause in return, or if all else fails, just a friend and a copy of this book will do! Then one of you can read the instructions while the other tackles the needles and yarn.

There are several methods of casting on; some methods give a stronger bottom edge than others, but every method starts with a slip knot. When casting on, make sure you keep the stitches loose.

CASTING ON WITH A SLIP KNOT – THE TWO-NEEDLE METHOD

The first stage to casting on is to make the first stitch by making a loop with a slip knot. Unwind the ball to give you approximately 12in (30cm) of yarn. Hold the yarn with your left hand with the tail hanging down and the ball of wool on your right.

With the right hand, wrap the yarn twice around your first two fingers, making a cross at the front in the middle of your fingers. Put the needle under the first loop (1), turn the needle so that it points down between your fingers, continue turning until the needle has done a 180 degree turn. Slip the loop off your fingers and on to the needle, gently tighten the stitch (2).

CASTING ON THE REST OF YOUR STITCHES

Make sure the needle with the slip knot is in your left hand. Slide the right needle up through the stitch, so it sits behind and the needles are crossed. Take the yarn in your right hand and wrap around the right needle from the back to the front (3). Pull your right needle back so the point comes down and catches the loop you have just made (4). Slip the new stitch off the right needle on to the left needle.

Don't be discouraged if you see…

The Novice Knitter

How to knit a stitch

So, well done, by hook or by crook you've managed to cast on those stitches. Now you need to get down to the "knitty gritty" and get going in earnest! Try putting on some music first. Knitting is just like playing an instrument. There are four moves to every knit stitch, so it's like a four-time beat.

As you knit, just keep on repeating "In, Around, Through and Off". Forget any mantras you were given at meditation classes and repeat this knitting chant instead.

IN (1):
Hold the yarn at the back. Slide the point of the right needle through the first loop, taking the tip of the right-hand needle so it sits in a cross behind the left.

AROUND (2):
Hold the needles with your left hand in a pinch. Pick up the yarn with your right hand and wrap it counter-clockwise around from the back of the right needle, through the middle of the cross. The yarn should now be at the front.

THROUGH (3):
Slide the right needle down and back through the stitch, making a loop on the right needle.

OFF (4):
Slip the original stitch off the left needle, leaving the newly formed stitch on the right needle.

How to purl a stitch

IN (1):
Hold the yarn at the front. Slide the right needle downwards through the first stitch on the left needle from right to left. Keep the needles crossed.

AROUND (2):
Using your right forefinger, take the yarn around the right needle in a counter-clockwise direction through the middle of the cross.

THROUGH (3):
Slide the right needle back up through the stitch, catching the yarn to create a loop on the right needle.

OFF (4):
Slip the original stitch off the left needle, leaving the newly formed stitch on the right needle.

At the end of every row, whether knit or purl, you will need to turn your work so you can start the next row. Hold the needle with all the stitches on the left and the right needle empty ready for you to begin the next row.

How to slip a stitch

In some patterns you will be required to slip a stitch. This is a method of passing a stitch from one needle to the other without knitting it.

With the right needle, using your IN chant, slip the right needle into the stitch on the left needle either "knitwise" or "purlwise" and OFF on to the right needle.

Garter stitch

This is created by using the knit stitch on every row. This produces an elastic piece of fabric and a construction that is perfect for learning to knit. Knitting a garter-stitch scarf (see page 74) for yourself or for the man in your life is an ideal first knitting project.

Stockinette stitch

This is the most common stitch. Whether knitting a sweater in one color or knitting a complicated Fairisle design, most patterns will be based on this stitch. Stockinette stitch consists of one row of knit and one row of purl. This produces a flat fabric with the stitches of your work looking like little "v"s, and makes counting stitches easy, as each "v" makes one stitch.

When you are knitting stockinette stitch, on a knit row you will have the little "v"s facing you and when you turn your work to purl, the little bumps on the other side will be facing you.

Right or wrong side?

The "right" side of your work will have the "v"s and the "wrong" side will have the bumps. This is important to remember when coming to the end of your garment when the next stage is to sew it up.

Right side   *Wrong side*

Rib

A classic-style sweater has a rib at the bottom and on the cuffs. Rib is more elastic than stockinette stitch and it will keep its shape better.

Ribbing consists of a sequence of knit and purl stitches in one row. The most common type of rib for cuffs and edgings is knit 1 st, purl 1 st and so on until the end of the row. Knit 2 sts, purl 2 sts makes a very elastic rib and is commonly used for scarves and hats. This stitch gives shaping to a garment that is designed to cling and show curves.

When ribbing, you need to remember to put your yarn to the back of your knitting for the knit stitch and bring it forward again for the purl stitch.

How to increase and decrease

Until you learn how to increase and decrease, you will be stuck with a square piece of fabric, which is only useful for scarves and blankets. So, to get to do those funky styles and garments that are shaped to fit the natural human form, you will have to shape up!

Remember that your arms are thinner at the bottom and wider at the top and the top of your torso is wider than your waist (well, sometimes!). Even a simple hat has to decrease at the top, unless some of you have square heads.

Increasing is usually done on the right side of the work. Patterns do not always give instructions on how to increase, as there are several methods. Increasing is also known as "making a stitch".

SIMPLE INCREASE

The simplest method is to work into the front and back of the same stitch. On a knit row, knit the stitch in, round and through, but don't take the stitch off (1). Instead, take the right needle, with the loop still on the left needle, and knit into the back of the stitch on the left needle (2). Slip the stitch off. You have now created an extra stitch.

On a purl row, purl into the front of the stitch as normal, but don't take the loop off the left needle. Purl into the back of the stitch on the left needle, creating the extra stitch.

SIMPLE DECREASE

The easiest way to decrease is by knitting or purling two stitches together at the same time. On a knit row, slide the right needle up through two stitches and knit them together as one stitch (3). This is called knit two together and is abbreviated in a pattern as k2tog. Use the same method for purling, only purl two stitches together.

Increasing

Decreasing

Casting off (binding off)

When casting off, you will usually be casting off an edge where you will pick up the stitches afterwards either to sew up or to make into a neckline. This means that it is vital to cast off loosely.

Knit the first two stitches on to the right-hand needle (1). Take the first stitch over the second, leaving one stitch on the needle (2). Knit the next stitch and draw the stitch already on the needle over it.

Always try to cast off on a knit row, but if you need to do it on a purl row, take the yarn back when you slip the second stitch over the first stitch and bring it back again to purl the next stitch.

When you get to the very last stitch, break the yarn, take the last stitch off the needle and thread the yarn through the loop and tighten.

If you need a really elastic cast-off edge, cast off in rib (1 stitch knit followed by 1 stitch purl).

Knitting a tension square

Once you have chosen your pattern, yarn and needles, the knitting drug will compel you to get started as soon as possible. But no matter how eager you feel, you must first knit a tension swatch. This determines the finished measurements of your garment. Many mistakes have been made owing to the lack of a swatch and the most beautiful garments have been passed over to the cat or dog basket because they are either too large or too small. Most patterns and yarn will give an ideal gauge.

Use the same needles, yarn and stitch as the pattern and knit a sample of at least 5in (12.5cm) square. Smooth out the piece on a flat surface without stretching it. Place a ruler horizontally on the work and mark 4in (10cm) with pins. Count the number of stitches between the pins. To check the row tension, put the ruler vertically on the work and mark 4in (10cm) with the pins. If you find you have more stitches or rows than the gauge in your pattern suggests, knit another swatch using larger needles, or if it is less try again with smaller needles.

> " Fashionable girls are turning to old-fashioned hobbies to ease the strain of urban life. Now knitting has replaced networking as the hippest after-hours occupation. "
>
> *Vogue, May 2004*

Joining yarn and changing colors

At some point the ball of wool will run out and you will need to join yarn. Whenever possible, join in new yarn at the beginning of a row. To measure if you have enough yarn to finish a row, measure across the row with the remaining yarn. If it reaches four times across the width, you will have enough for a stockinette-stitch row.

Slide your right needle into the first stitch. Place the new yarn over the old yarn and bring it between the two needles with the tail end to the left side. Make sure you leave a tail approximately 4in (10cm) long.

Bring your yarn up from under the existing yarn and knit with the new yarn, so that both types of yarn have twisted together at the back. Make sure you leave sufficient yarn to sew in.

After you've done a few stitches, stop and tie the ends in a knot – they can be sewn into the seam later.

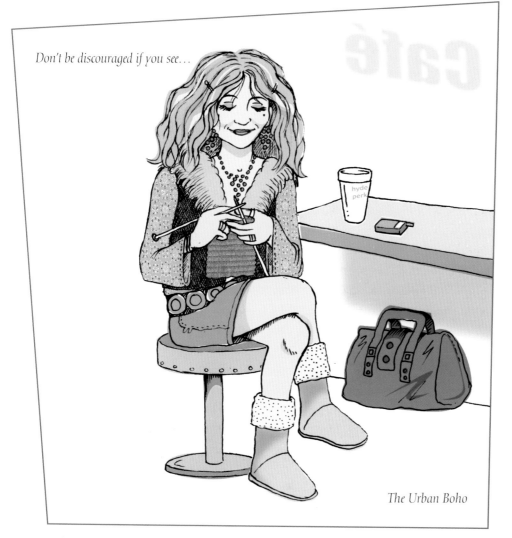

Don't be discouraged if you see...

The Urban Boho

How to read a knitting pattern

Once you've tuned into the knitting lingo, it's just like following a cookery recipe. But let's dismiss that analogy in case you knit a cabbage sweater. Like a recipe, however, always read the pattern through first so you get an idea of how the design and techniques fit into place.

The beginning of each pattern will have the sizing and the materials you need to knit with.

SIZING

The smallest sizes of the item you're knitting will be printed first and the larger sizes will follow on.

To fit bust:					
32	34	36	38	40	in
81	86	91	97	102	cm

Just to confuse things, you will sometimes be given the actual size measurement of the garment. This is the actual size that it will knit to, rather than the measurement of the person who will be wearing it. Remember that most knitted garments won't be as tight-fitting as a bra, so you will need a bit of space to get into it. Following the size, you will have the measurement of the garment's length and its sleeve seam length. Remember that if you need to adjust the length, you may need extra yarn.

Bust measurement: the measurement of the bust/chest is taken under the arms. Ask someone you fancy to help you out – it's good for breaking the ice on a first date.

Back measurement: this is the length from the back of the neck to the very bottom edge of the garment.

Sleeve measurement: this is from the edge of the cuff to the widest point, which is just below your armpit.

The pattern may show these measurements in a diagram.

MATERIALS

Yarn amounts are also shown at the beginning of the pattern, underneath the measurements so you can calculate the amount of yarn needed to knit the pattern.

To fit bust:					
32	34	36	38	40	in
81	86	91	97	102	cm
Yarn:					
10	10	11	12	13	balls

Make quite sure you have bought the correct amount of yarn and if you are substituting a yarn, make sure it has the equivalent weight, yardage or meterage. Sometimes it's wise to overbuy a little to avoid running out of yarn. Most good yarn suppliers will let you have a refund on unopened balls or skeins of wool. If you have an accommodating supplier, they may be able to put yarn aside for you and you can buy it as and when you need it. This ensures you get the right dye-lot number for the yarn you have chosen. (Don't expect them to keep it for the sweater that you've been working on for the past 18 years, though.)

In the materials section of the pattern you will also find the recommended needle size and any other equipment that's needed, such as buttons, beads, cable needles, crochet hooks or stitch holders.

KNITTING INSTRUCTIONS YARDAGE

It can sometimes be confusing to read through the pattern before you begin. This is because it will only become obvious once you start knitting, so don't start thinking you're totally dumb or that the pattern is useless!

Knitting instructions give the smallest size first and the larger sizes follow within parentheses. So, for example, cast on 96 (100: 106: 110: 116). Follow the order according to the size you are knitting throughout. It's useful to go through the pattern with a highlighter marker pen so you don't read the wrong size by mistake.

Asterisks or parentheses are used to indicate the repetition of a sequence of stitches. So, for example, "*K1, p2; rep from * to end" means that you must repeat the sequence inside the asterisks until you get to the end of the row. This instruction can also be written in parentheses, as "(K1, p2) to end". To confuse you even more, asterisks and parentheses are sometimes used together. For example "*K1, p2 (K2, p1) 3 times; rep from * to end". The parenthetical instruction means that these stitches only are to be repeated three times before returning to the instructions immediately after the asterisk. So, following the example, you knit 1, pearl 2 and then knit 2 and pearl 1 three times, and then go back to the beginning of the sequence until the end of the row. Confused? Well, just start knitting and it will become more obvious.

It is always good to have a pencil in hand to make sure you repeat the sequence the exact number of times specified. Some knitters have a pin neatly attached to the pattern page and make little points instead of pencil marks.

If you have to put your knitting down in a hurry to answer the phone or the doorbell, always take the time to mark where you are on the pattern or you will end up having to take the row back because you've forgotten where you are. The salesman at the door isn't worth losing stitches over.

The phrase "work straight" means continue knitting without increasing or decreasing, until instructed.

'COZ MAKING UP IS HARD TO DO

Making up is always a good thing. Sometimes over a cup of coffee or a romantic meal, but in knitting terms it means putting the whole thing together. Always follow the recommended sequence in the pattern; it will be there for a reason (see page 39 for sewing-up instructions).

ABBREVIATIONS

The next hurdle is to understand the pattern abbreviations. They are not as bad as they look. You won't need to memorize them because they are usually at the beginning or the end of most pattern books. You will find them at the beginning of the patterns section (see page 51).

> "Knitting, if you choose, can be at the heart of a fulfilling and creative way of living."
>
> *Weekend Knitting: 50 Unique Projects and Ideas*

Fairisle patterns

Fairisle is the technique used for working with more than one color. At some point you just won't be able to resist having a go, as there are so many wonderful patterns that you can add to your knitting repertoire. So don't be scared of the big "F" word, Fairisle.

Fairisle takes a little more concentration than one-color knitting, so turn off the TV, allow yourself a spot of time and don't answer the phone. Fairisle works better in stockinette stitch where the design shows at the front of the work and the yarn is carried along at the back.

In most knitting instruction manuals the Fairisle techniques "stranding" and "weaving" are explained. These explanations can be enough to drive any novice knitter to the nearest bonfire to burn their bamboo needles, so some easier methods are outlined here.

OVER AND UNDER
If you are knitting a design that has less than four stitches in one color, use the over-and-under method.

So, for example:
1. Knit with the first color yarn.
2. When you want to bring in a new color, drop the first color and bring the 2nd color over the 1st color and start knitting with it.

Your yarns can get very tangled as they wind around themselves and it can take just as much time untangling yarn as it does knitting the garment, so if you alternate the over and under to under and over every time you do a color change, you'll find the yarn gets less messed up. There are several tips to keeping colors from tangling. Some people divide the balls of yarn and put them into separate jelly jars. I find you still have to move the jelly jars around all over the place and then as soon as you move for a cup of coffee you knock them over and spend all your time chasing the balls around the room, putting them back in the jars.

TWISTING
If you are knitting with more than three stitches use the twisting method, the best method for carrying along the color you're not using. It also keeps the knitting from getting too tight and puckering up.

Knit with the first color yarn (color A). Join in the 2nd color (color B) (1). After 2 or 3 stitches, pick up yarn A and twist it around yarn B at the back and continue knitting with yarn B. Just keep twisting when you want to change colors. In this way your yarn will be carried behind the work and will avoid forming long loops (the pieces of yarn that get carried behind your work) (2). The loops can look ugly if too long and can catch in fingers or hands. If you twist on every stitch, your work will bunch up and look ugly. If you twist every three stitches, your work will lay flat and still allow the fabric to stretch.

When you get to the end of a row, just before your last stitch, twist your yarn so your second color extends to the end of the row.

HOW TO READ A FAIRISLE PATTERN
The easy answer is "carefully". Most Fairisle patterns are worked from a chart, which can take a bit of getting used to. Choose a simple design in two colors to start off with (such as the cell phone/iPod cover on page 70).

 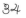

A chart will give a single pattern repeat of the complete design on a squared grid. Either colors or symbols will represent the colors. Work from the bottom to the top. Horizontally, each square represents a stitch and vertically each square represents a row.

For a stockinette-stitch pattern:
Knit rows – read the chart from right to left.
Purl rows – read the chart from left to right.

When you have completed one row, follow the row that is immediately above the last. Keep a pencil or a row counter near by and mark off the rows as you complete them.

Often, only one repeat of the pattern is shown and you will have to repeat this pattern across the row. There will be bold vertical lines to show the area that is to be repeated. The stitches at either side of these lines show the edge stitches to be worked at the beginning and the end of the work.

Follow the pattern exactly. I'll repeat that: follow the pattern exactly. And for those of you looking after young children: follow the pattern exactly. Constantly check your work after every few stitches and every row. If you have gone wrong, don't continue in the hope it will work out. It won't. Undo the incorrect stitches and correct the mistakes.

Don't be discouraged if you see…

The country living knitter

Troubleshooting — or the knitting-disaster hall of fame

Here is a quick problem-solving guide to common mistakes when knitting.

'OOPS, I'VE DROPPED A STITCH'
It's so easy to do. Everyone does it, so it is essential that you know how to pick up dropped stitches.

Picking up stitches on a knit row
Hold your knitting with the right side (knit side) facing (1). Put the tip of the right needle into the dropped stitch from front to back, to stop it running any further. Then pick up the horizontal strand of yarn, so it sits above the stitch (2). With your left needle, lift the picked-up stitch over the horizontal strand and slip it off the needle (3). Transfer the stitch on to the left needle and knit to the end of the row (4).

Picking up stitches on a purl row
Hold your knitting with the wrong side (purl side) facing (5). Put the tip of the right needle into the dropped stitch from back to front. Pick up the horizontal strand of yarn, so it sits above the stitch (6). With your left needle, lift the picked-up stitch over the horizontal strand and slip it off the needle (7). Transfer the stitch on to the left (8).

RUNS
If the dropped stitch creates a run going down several rows, either pick up the stitch in the usual way, picking up from the bottom to the top, or instead use a crochet hook.

Work with the dropped stitch at the front of the knitting (9). Put the crochet hook into the stitch from front to back. Loop the horizontal strand with the crochet hook and pull it through the stitch (10). Continue up the run and when you reach the top, hook the stitch on to the left needle – then you can cheer.

TWIST AND SHOUT, OR TWISTED STITCHES
Twisted stitches are created either when dropped stitches have been picked up the wrong way round or when the yarn has been taken the wrong way round the needle.

On a knit row: knit into the back of the stitch.
On a purl row: purl into the back of the stitch.

UNDOING STITCHES

This is always a frustrating activity. Having gone to all the time and trouble knitting, the last thing you want is to have to unravel it. It's a bit like taking the wrong turn up the highway and having to drive 10 miles to the next exit and 20 miles back to get to where you wanted.

Undoing stitches stitch by stitch

If your mistake is on the same row or only one row down, you may need to unravel your knitting stitch by stitch.

Put your yarn at the back with the right side facing you. Put the left needle from front to back through the stitch below the stitch you want to unravel that's on the right needle (1). Pull the right needle back and let the stitch slip off the needle and pull the yarn (2).

For a purl row, you should use the same method but with the wrong side facing and the yarn at the front.

Unravelling rows

Try to avoid this, but you may need to take off several rows if you have failed to correct a mistake by picking up individual stitches.

Put your knitting on a flat surface and pull the needle away and off the stitches. With one hand on the knitting to keep it flat, pull the yarn with the other hand, and gently undo the amount of rows needed. Make sure you count the rows and allow for any decreasing or increasing that you have made. Deduct the rows off your row counter.

When you have undone as many rows as required, put the stitches back on the needle with a smaller size needle. Start knitting again as normal, using your original size needles.

WHAT ROW AM I ON?

Even though the house may be completely quiet and you are convinced you won't be disturbed, there will inevitably come a moment when you will innocently put your knitting down. Then, when you get back to it, you'll have to work out what row you were on.

This is where the importance of the classic knitters' phrase, "I've just got to finish this row!" comes into play. When you put your work down in the middle of a row, it's an easy mistake to pick it up and start knitting the wrong way. Always make sure your yarn is on the right of your work and try to finish a row before going off to make a coffee or answering the phone (and remember to mark on your pattern the stage you have reached!).

If you do lose your place, when you pick up the knitting again hold your two needles and see where your yarn is. Whether it's at the front or the back, it should always be worked with the yarn coming from the top stitch on the right needle. If the yarn is coming out from the left needle, simply turn the knitting around and continue your work.

Picking up stitches for borders

To prevent the edge of the knitted fabric from curling, most knitted pieces will have an edging or border, either sewn on or created by picking up stitches. In the pattern instructions this may be referred to as "pick up and knit" or "knit up". The pattern will tell you how many stitches are to be picked up.

PICKING UP ON A CAST-ON/CAST-OFF EDGE USING ONE NEEDLE

With the right side facing you, put the right needle from the front to the back under both loops (1). Wind the yarn round the needle and in a knit action draw the loop through to create a new stitch on the needle (2). Continue to pick up the amount of stitches specified in the pattern.

PICKING UP ALONG A SIDE EDGE

With the right side facing and with one needle in your right hand, pick up the stitches one stitch in from the edge. This ensures a neater edge and keeps your work tidy.

It is useful to mark out the number of stitches you need evenly along the length of fabric with pins. Measure the distance along the edge and divide it by the number of stitches you are instructed to pick up.

Knitting buttonholes

Buttonholes on knitted garments do not always create the neatest of holes. This doesn't matter, however, as you can neaten them with a blanket stitch later. The fun is in choosing the buttons to pretty up your knitted item.

Knit until you get to the part in the pattern where you need the buttonhole. Cast off the amount of stitches specified in the pattern (this depends on the size of the buttonhole and the thickness of your yarn) (1). Knit to the end of the row. On your next row, knit to the point where your cast-off stitches are. Turn your work by switching your needles; put the left needle in the right hand and the right needle in the left hand. Cast on the same number of stitches as you cast off. Turn your work again and work to the end (2).

Sewing in ends

If possible, sew in the yarn ends as you go along and certainly before you make up the garment, otherwise you'll end up with all the loose ends tangled up in the seams as you're sewing up. Thread the loose end into a yarn-sewing needle. Sew in and out through the bars of the stitch on the wrong side of the work and cut them loosely so the yarn doesn't unravel. Stitches can be darned either vertically or horizontally, whichever looks neater. If you ignore this advice, the back of your garment will end up looking like a bird's nest.

Sewing up or making up

This can also be called "knitting, sewing and kittens…" Once you've knitted your garment, you then need to sew it together, but you're having kittens at the thought… At this point I used to just hand my knitted pieces over to my mother, so I never felt the satisfaction of finishing it all by myself. She eventually got fed up and made me sew up on my own. Many knitters give up just before it comes to sewing up, throw the knitted pieces together in a bag and abandon it in the attic. But don't panic, it's incredibly satisfying to see the pieces all coming together, so just take your time and breathe…

Place the pieces on a flat surface, putting them next to each other so you can see the shape of the garment, right side up. Pin the pieces together very loosely. Safety pins are more suitable than straight pins, which tend to get lost in the knitted fabric. Pin the corners first and fill in the other bits after. Keep checking and double-checking that you have it all the right way round, as the most frustrating thing is to start sewing and find that you have sewn a right side to a wrong side and a wrong side to a right side. Use the same yarn as your knitted fabric for the sewing up, unless it's a particularly weak or bulky yarn, in which case match up the color with a thinner and stronger yarn.

> " Mrs Moon
> sitting up in the sky
> little old lady
> rock-a-bye
> with a ball of fading light
> and silvery needles
> knitting the night
>
> Mother by Prabha Raj
> As a pair of needles
> Criss cross,
> I see her thoughts
> Setting her wrinkles
> To play.
>
> The moment she completes
> The picking of stitches,
> Her wrinkles
> Erase out
>
> I call it
> The juxtaposition of
> Mind and sentiment. "

Roger McGough, Mrs Moon

SEWING SEAMS

There are a number of techniques for joining seams. Start with the over-and-over method and try the others later when you are more confident.

Over-and-over method

This is the easiest method of joining seams, although not always the neatest. It gives a nice flat seam.

Thread sufficient yarn to sew up the whole seam. Put right side to right side, with a wrong side facing you. Starting at the bottom edge, put the needle from the back of your two pieces of fabric to the front. Take the needle over to the back and put the needle from back to front into the next stitch. Go back to the original first stitch and put the needle from back to front and pull it through. This secures the first stitch (1). Match corresponding stitches from both sides, put the needle into the top of the stitches through both pieces of fabric from the back and pull through to the front. Take the needle over and put in again from the back to the front as before. Continue by spacing the stitches approximately every two rows (2).

Beginning a seam for back stitch and mattress stitch

There are the first few stitches that hold the fabric together and secure the yarn so the sewing doesn't come undone.

Begin by putting both fabrics right side to right side, with the wrong side facing you. Use the long tail left from your cast-on row, or thread another piece of yarn into your sewing needle. Put the needle from back to front through the corner stitch of both pieces

of knitting. Secure the yarn by putting the needle back up through the same hole (3).

Back stitch

This, the simplest of all sewing-up stitches, is suitable for seams and for yarn up to double-knitting thickness. This method produces a neat seam, but it can be bulky if used with thicker yarn.

Pin the right sides together with the wrong side facing you, pinning the sides together row for row (4). Begin your seam (as above), with the yarn finishing at the front. Put the needle into the work just behind where the last stitch came out and make a short stitch, bringing the needle back to the front (5). Put the needle back into where the previous stitch ended and make a long stitch, so the needle comes out about a stitch in front of where the last stitch ended (6). Keep repeating this process until the end. It will make a continuous line of stitches of a similar length on the side of the work facing you.

> " Knit on, with confidence and hope, through all crises. "
>
> *Elizabeth Zimmermann*

Mattress stitch on stockinette stitch

This is one of the neatest stitches to use. It takes a bit longer, but its almost invisible and makes a completely straight seam.

Begin your seam. With the right sides of your knitting facing each other, put your needle under the first two running bars, and pull it through. (The bars are the pieces of yarn between each "v" shape on the knit side (1).) Pass the needle under the first two bars on the other piece of fabric and pull it through. Don't pull your fabrics too close together at this point and leave your stitches quite loose – you will pull them together later (2). Put the needle into the same place that it came out of on the right-hand piece of fabric. Pick up the next two running bars, put the needle to the same point where it came out on the left-hand piece of fabric, and come up two bars on the same side (3). When you have sewn 4 or 5 stitches, gently pull your yarn to draw the edges together and it will become invisible (4).

Joining two cast-off edges

This is a slight variation on mattress stitch and also creates a neat seam.

Begin your seam. With the right sides facing and working from right to left, put the needle through the center of your first stitch underneath the cast-off stitch and pull it through. At this stage, don't pull your stitches tight, as this will be done later (5). Put your needle through the center of the stitch corresponding on the opposite side and bring it out in the center of the next stitch along (6). Put the needle into the center of the next stitch along on the other side and back up through the center of the next stitch along (7). Repeat until the end of the seam. When you have sewn 4 stitches, pull gently in the same way as with mattress stitch (8).

Washing, blocking and steaming (finishing your project)

Pressing your fabric can make the difference between it looking like a professional piece of art or an old rag you've found in a dumpster.

Yarn that has a high content of natural fiber can be pressed, but some yarn can be totally ruined by a hot iron. Check the label on the yarn for details of whether your yarn can be pressed. It should give you all the information you need, even the temperature at which the iron should be set. It will also tell you if you need to use a dry cloth or a damp cloth. Often you will find pressing instructions at the end of your pattern.

DAMP FINISHING

If you are instructed that the yarn is not to be pressed, then follow the method below.

Find a damp and colorfast towel (not the one you've just used for drying the dog). Lay your pieces of fabric on the damp towel and then roll them up loosely together. Leave for approximately one hour for the knitting to absorb the dampness from the towel.

Undo the towel on a flat surface and place the pieces once more on top of it. Pin the pieces into shape (this is blocking).

Find another damp cloth and lay it over the top so your fabric is sandwiched. Press gently down on to your fabric so every part is touching the cloth and leave it to dry somewhere where it's not going to stay damp for too long – otherwise it will start to smell.

BLOCKING

This is a method used to keep your garment in shape while it is drying. Blocking is sometimes also used to pin a garment out before sewing it up, especially when some knitted fabrics are prone to curling at the edges. It is a good way of shaping motifs and Fairisle, which can look uneven occasionally.

It's best to get as much moisture out of the knitted fabric as possible before laying it out. You can wrap it in a towel and then put it in the washing machine for a very short spin. Alternatively, wrap the item in a towel and press it gently to absorb as much water into the towel as possible. This is a great method for getting rid of any lingering angst, but don't press it too tight. Remember that you're only getting rid of excess water!

Before you start blocking, remember how the piece is supposed to look. Reshape the pieces and lay them out on a dry towel. Pin out your pieces with large-headed colored pins or large safety pins. Use a padded surface or, failing that, a nice thick towel. Gently ease the fabric into place to get the correct measurements and lay on the wrong side. Place the pins approximately 1in (2.5cm) apart on the very edge of the fabric.

PRESSING

Pressing helps the fabric hold its shape. The label should give you pressing instructions. As a rule, any natural yarn and cotton and linen can be pressed with a damp cloth. Steam irons are also an asset, as they can be used over a cloth and don't need to actually touch the knitting so won't flatten it in any way. Synthetic yarn should not be pressed. For yarn mixtures that have some natural and some synthetic fibers, press with a cool iron over a dry cloth. However, never use steam on acrylic, as it goes "dead" and sloppy. A great investment is a Teflon or non-stick cover for your iron that makes it glide over the knitting, allowing the steam to come out of the iron without scorching. Turn on the iron and check the correct temperature. Place the damp or dry cloth over

Blocking – before

Blocking – after

the pinned-out pieces of knitting. Hover the iron over the damp cloth so it makes it steam; don't drag the iron over the fabric or it will become misshapen. Do not press any ribbed edges. Remove some of the pins and, if the work stays flat, take the rest of the pins out and leave to dry. If the edges are still curling when you have taken some of the pins out, you need to repin it and leave it to dry with the pins in. Once you have finished sewing up your garment, press it again along the seams using the same method, only this time without any pinning.

WASHING

Washing a hand-knitted garment can be a terrifying thought when you have other clothes that have been tinted with dye that has run in the wash. And the last thing you need is to spend all that tender loving care on knitting and finishing your garment, only to have it shrink to such a minute state that you have to donate it to the elves' section of a charity store.

The most important thing is to read the yarn label. This tends to read like a cryptic code, so a few hints follow to help you out.

Hand-washing

Use lukewarm water and a mild soap washing agent. There are various liquid handwashing products on the market and I prefer to use these as the powder takes more time to dissolve and some don't dissolve so well in mild temperatures. Don't rub the knitted fabric, but gently squeeze it to loosen any dirt. Do not leave your knitted garment to soak – it's best to get it washed and dried in the shortest possible time. Let the water out of the sink before lifting the garment out and gently squeeze the water out when the sink is empty.

The garment may be very heavy when filled with water and lifting it out of the water may stretch it. Lay the garment on a towel and roll it up loosely. Then take another towel, lay the garment out and reshape the garment to its correct measurements. Leave the piece to dry naturally away from direct sunlight, and don't be tempted to put it on the radiator.

Note: You can spin some knitted yarn, such as cotton and linen, in the washing machine on a slow and gentle cycle.

Machine washing

Check the yarn label to find out if your yarn is machine washable. Use the instructions and set the machine on the recommended temperature. If you are nervous about the item stretching, put the item in a pillowcase inside the drum of the machine. In times of extreme agitation, revert to handwashing! Then lay out the garment to dry. Don't put it in the dryer.

Dry cleaning

If the label says "dry clean", dry clean only. Make sure your dry cleaner doesn't put it on a hanger and doesn't press it. Take the yarn label in for them to check. Remember, this is your masterpiece.

> **"**In the rhythm of the needles,
> there is music for the soul.**"**

Text from a sampler

Beading

Beading can make the difference between a well-executed and worthy piece of knitting and a really jazzed-up little number. It can give a real quality finish to cuffs and borders and can make bags and purses look delectably classy.

Threading beads on to the yarn is a fairly complicated activity, but a strangely satisfying one. You may imagine that you can just thread them straight on to the yarn needle and then straight on to the yarn… but think again. Most beads don't have a huge hole and won't go on the yarn needle, so first of all find yourself a thin sewing needle.

Make sure you buy beads that have a big enough hole to fit on a sewing needle. You'll be surprised at the size of bead holes once you start looking and some people can get quite obsessed about it. If you find yourself mumbling "Hmmm… preciousssssss" in triumph and delight when you find the right one, just like Golum in *The Lord of the Rings*, it's time to seek medical help.

THREADING BEADS

This needs to be done before you start knitting. Double-thread your sewing needle with a piece of thread so the loop hangs down. Then thread your yarn through the loop, leaving a tail approximately 6in (15cm) long. Thread the bead over the needle and push it down to the end of the thread until you get to the yarn, then continue to push it over the yarn beyond the tail until it is on a single yarn thread.

Thread as many beads as you require on to the yarn. It is better to thread more than you need rather than less, because once you start knitting you can't add more beads without breaking the yarn and rethreading them (1).

There are several methods for knitting with beads; this one seems most logical, and once you get started it all becomes obvious.

Knit to the point where the bead is required. Put the right needle into the stitch. Bring one of the beads up the yarn until it meets the work, so it is in position (2). Knit into the next stitch and push the bead through the stitch to the right side of your work (3). Pull the yarn firmly in place (4).

On a purl row, repeat the method as for the knit row, but push the bead through to the right side.

Dazzling Decorations

All knitters have bags or baskets full of end-bits of yarn left over from the previous project – and some knitting packrats also keep hoards of beads. Don't let these valuable materials go to waste; they can make a huge difference to a plain piece of knitting. The following decorations are perfect fun items to adorn your cushions, sweaters, bags, hats or scarves.

Pom-poms

Pom-poms can liven up a cushion, throw, hat, scarf or dog jacket. Try using strands of yarn different colors of to make multi-colored ones. When you have used up one color, just change to a different color.

Cut out two circles of card (an empty cereal box will do nicely) to the size you want your pom-pom to be, using a glass or other circular utensil as a guide (1). Cut a small hole in the center of each circle (2). Place the two circles together. Wind some yarn off a ball to make a small ball. Put the tail through the small circle and start winding it round the cards through the hole, until the hole is so small that you can't get any more yarn through (3). For a thinner pom-pom, use less yarn. When the last piece of yarn is used up, with both index fingers pull the yarn apart at the outer circle to reveal the card. Insert scissors between the two pieces of card. Holding the tail of yarn with your left hand, cut round the outer edge of the pom-pom (4). When you have cut all the way around, wind a separate piece of yarn between the two pieces of card. Secure very tightly in a double knot (5). Remove the two cards and trim the pom-pom.

Don't be discouraged if you see...

The hippy knitter

Tassels

These look great on the corners of cushions or on the top of hats.

Find a cassette or CD case, or something solid the required length of the tassel. Wrap your yarn round the CD case 30 or 40 times, depending on the thickness of the wool and how fat you want the tassel to be (1). Cut the yarn at the bottom. Take a separate piece of yarn and thread it through the top of the wool on the CD case. Tie very tight with a double knot (2). Pull all the wool off the CD case. Holding the top of the tassel with your left hand, take some scissors and cut the bottom to form tassels (3).

Cut a separate piece of yarn. Tie the yarn around the tassel and make a neck, wrapping the yarn round the tassel several times. Secure with a double knot (4). Thread the same piece of yarn on a sewing needle and push the needle from front to back several times to secure (5). Trim the bottom.

Fringes

Fringes are perfect for scarves or any other garment to give them a more glamorous appearance.

Find a cassette or CD case, or something solid the required length of the fringe. Wrap your yarn round the CD case 4 or 5 times, depending on the thickness of the wool and how fat you want the fringe to be (1).

Slide the wool off the CD case, holding it tightly at the top. Push the fringe up through the bottom loop of the knitted item, using either your fingers or a crochet hook (2). Making a loop with the fringe, push the bottom of the tassel though it, and pull tight (3). Trim the bottom.

Knitted bow

This pretty bow is made from five pieces of ribbed knitting.

Make the two loops from two pieces of ribbing 22 sts wide and 5$\frac{1}{2}$in (14cm) long. The two pointed ends are made by casting on 2 sts and then increasing in the first stitch of every other row until 22 sts are on the needle. Then knit straight until the end measures 5$\frac{1}{2}$in (14cm). The middle strap is made with 16 sts and 2$\frac{1}{2}$in (6.5cm) of ribbed knitting. (K1, P1).

To make up, fold the pieces for the loops in half, pleat them so they look neat, and sew them securely. Pleat the straight ends of the pointed pieces and sew to the loops. Wrap the small strip to form the knot and the bow is complete.

Knitted flower

Knit this flower with any yarn, using the needles recommended for the yarn. It can be used to add extra glamour to bags, hats and scarves – or simply put a safety pin in the back and use it as a brooch.

Cast on 8 sts.
Row 1: slip 1, knit 7
Row 2: slip 1, knit 5 (2 sts remain on left needle), turn and put yarn to the back.
Row 3: slip 1, knit 3 (2 sts remain on left needle), turn and put yarn to the back.
Row 4: slip 1, knit 3, turn.
Row 5: slip 1, knit 5 (0 sts remain on left needle), turn.

Row 6: slip 1, knit 6 (leaving 1 st on left needle), turn.
Row 7: slip 1 and begin casting off until 1 st remains, turn.
Cast on 7 sts.

Repeat 5 times (to create 6 petals).
Cast off last sts leaving a long tail.
Thread yarn on a wool-sewing needle and sew first petal to last petal creating a flower shape.
Weave sewing needle in and out of each petal along inside edge of hole and gently pull yarn together, closing hole.
Sew in ends.

PART THREE

Cool girl's patterns...

... funky fashions

Keeping Up with the Bridget Joneses

Because we all now lead such pressured, busy lives, knitting activities are most popularly focused on quick projects that can easily be accommodated between other commitments.

In the patterns section that follows (see pages 52–92), projects have been chosen that use basic but interesting techniques and that incorporate the new attractive yarns that have played a strong part in drawing knitters back to the craft over the past few years. Yarns have been selected from fashionable yarn suppliers who have responded to the fact that new knitters are constantly inspired by yarn color and variety and so consequently change and update the yarns available in order to meet new trends in knitting. You'll find chunky knits and cottons from Rowan; hand-dyed chunky, ribbon and fluffy yarn from Colinette; the latest Alpaca Silk, Cashmere, and Merino yarn from the Debbie Bliss collection.

Knitwear is being shown in all the latest designer collections and some versions of designer garments have been included in simplified form to make them easy to knit – the results are chic and professional looking. These patterns will help you practice your techniques and will lead you on to more advanced knitting. Two of the designers who have contributed projects, Vikki Haffenden and Jane Rota, both work in the Fashion and Textile Department of Brighton University in the UK. Their expertise in knitwear fashion and their street-level understanding of what fashion students are wearing have helped them produce some of the really fantastic garments.

The cell phone cover (see page 70) was suggested by the author's teenage daughter, Maddy. She and her friends loved the idea of having something individual and fun in which to carry their phones. After all, cell phones are generally pretty gray and boring for a color-loving teenager; it's a pity that corporate gray cars can't be given the same treatment!

The dog jackets (see page 83) were an inspiration from Roger Perkins, an avid dog lover who can always be relied on for an original and amusing idea. Why dress your dog in a boring plastic jacket when the "must haves" this season in the doggy world of fashion are shark fins and pom-poms?

There are also two sewing projects, still with knitting in mind. Just as an apprentice metalworker or gunsmith used to make the tools he would need for his craft, we've put together projects for a yarn tote bag (see page 90) and a needle case using fake cow fur (see page 92).

Other projects demonstrate how individual yarn qualities, as well as accessories and textures, can turn a plain knitted garment into something individual and special. The designer of the chunky tasseled scarf (see page 74) fell in love with the hand-dyed yarn, designed a simple, basic scarf and turned it into a crowd stopper. Also included in the patterns that follow are pom-poms (see page 80 & 83), tassels (see page 81), and knitted flowers (see page 78). The current trend for ribbons, buttons and beads has also been an inspiration, so start rummaging in your local charity stores or in your nearest craft store to find vintage or interesting ones. The design of the button handbag with its ribbon and buttons (see page 82) is, literally, straight from the catwalk and because it has no shaping, it's a delight to knit. The patterns are designed to be adaptable so you can easily change the accessories and styling to personalize your item.

There are plenty of designs that are ideal first projects. The easy sweater (see page 52) is just what it says: a cozy style that's a joy to wear. The scarves, hats and bags are also perfect items to practice simple stitching techniques. The pattern for the motif on the cell phone cover (see page 70) uses the Fairisle technique (see pages 34/35) and the motif on the Dare-to-wear bikini (see page 68) uses the intarsia technique. The make-up bag (see page 78) is a glamorous little number giving you the chance to have a shot at some beading.

Don't be discouraged by abbreviations as they are all explained opposite. And if you drop a stitch, just turn to pages 36/37 for guidance. Refer, also, to the list of suppliers on page 95.

Remember: every great garment begins with a first stitch and the making is as much fun as the wearing.

Abbreviations

alt	alternate		ptbl	purl through back loop
beg	begin(ning)		p2tog	purl two stitches together
bo	bind off (cast off)		r	row
cm	centimeter		rem	remaining
cn	cable needle		rep	repeat
co	cast on		rept	repeat
cont	continue		rs	right side
dec	decrease		rev st st	reverse stockinette stitch
dk	double knitting		sk	skip
dpn	double pointed needle		skpo	slip one, knit one, pass slipped stitch over
foll	following		sl	slip
fwd	forward		sl l	slip one
g st	garter stitch		Ssk	slip one knitwise, slip one knitwise, knit two together putting left hand needle into the front of the right hand needle's stitches.
in; ins	inches			
inc	increase			
incl	including		Ssp	slip one knitwise, slip one knitwise, return to left hand needle and purl two together upwards through back of sts
K	knit			
k1	knit one			
K2tog	knit two stitches together		st	stitch
m1	make one		sts	stitches
mb	make bobble		st st	stockinette stitch
mm	millimeter		tbl	through back of loop
no	number		tog	together
oz	ounce		ws	wrong side
patt	pattern		wyb	with yarn in back
P	purl		wyf	with yarn in front
p1	purl one		yb	yarn back
pb	place bead		yf	yarn forward
pfb	purl into the front and the back of the stitch		yfwd	yarn forward
pnso	pass next stitch over		yo	yarn over
psso	pass slipped stitch over		yrn	yarn round needle

The easy sweater

This oversize unisex sweater is amazingly quick to knit in garter stitch. The yarn is really luxurious – as I was knitting it my thoughts wandered from atmospheric views of Paris and the Seine and fashion catwalks to the tempting sights and smells of croissants, coffee, and champagne.

EQUIPMENT
1 pair #11 needles
1 darning needle

YARN
10–11 x 100g balls Rowan Polar Wool, shade 645 Winter White

TENSION
Using #11 needles with stockinette stitch 12 sts x 16 rows = 4in (10cm) square.
Using #11 needles with garter stitch 12 sts x 20 rows = 4in (10cm) square.

SIZING
To fit chest sizes: 36/38/40in (92/97/102cm)
Final knitted size: 44/46/48in (112/117/122cm)

METHOD
Back
Cast on 68/70/72 sts.

Row 1: Knit 1 row into back of stitch.
Row 2: Purl 1 row.
Row 3: Knit 1 row.
Row 4: Purl 1 row.
Row 5: Knit 1 row.
Row 6: Purl 1 row.
These 6 rows form the curled edging.
Knit 70/71/72 rows or until work measures 14$\frac{1}{2}$/14$\frac{3}{4}$/15in (37/37.5/38cm.)
(just knit and no purl for garter stitch)

Decrease 2 sts at beginning of the next 2 rows.
Knit 71/72/73 rows or until work measures 27/27$\frac{1}{4}$/27$\frac{1}{2}$in (68.5/69/69.5cm).
Cast off.

Front
Cast on 68/70/72 sts.
Knit 1 row into back of stitch.
Knit 5 rows stockinette stitch.

Knit 70/71/72 rows or until work measures 14$\frac{1}{2}$/14$\frac{3}{4}$/15in (37/37.5/38cm).
Decrease 2 sts at beginning of next 2 rows.
Knit 16 rows.
Knit 32/33/34 turn. Slip remaining stitches on to a spare needle.
Knit 32/33/34 sts.
Knit 32/33/34 sts and turn.
K2tog and continue to end.
Continue knitting like this and K2tog at the neck edge at beginning of every 4th row until work measures 27/27$\frac{1}{4}$/27$\frac{1}{2}$in (68.5/69/69.5cm) .
Cast off.
Return to the stitches held on the spare needle and knit from the neck edge, rejoining yarn.
Knit 32/33/34 sts.
Knit 32/33/34 sts.
K2tog and continue to end of row.
Continue knitting like this and k2tog at the neck edge at beginning of every 4th row until work measures 27/27$\frac{1}{4}$/27$\frac{1}{2}$in (68.5/69/69.5cm).
Cast off.

Sleeves
Cast on 31/33/35 sts.
Knit 1 row into back of stitch.
Knit 5 rows stockinette stitch.
Knit 84 rows or until work measures 17in (43cm),

increasing 1 stitch at each end of every 4 rows. Cast off.

Making up

Join shoulder seams.

Join sleeves to the main body of the garment.

Join side seams.

Join sleeve seams.

Sew in any ends.

Steam garment to shape gently.

Adding the neck trim

1. With the right side facing you and beginning at a shoulder, pick up and knit 21 (don't worry if you have 1 or 2 extra or 1 or 2 fewer stitches, but do keep looking at the stitches you are picking up to check they look fairly neat).

2. Knit 5 rows of stockinette stitch and cast off.

3. Repeat for the other side of the neck edge.

4. Then pick up and knit 22 sts across the back neck. Knit 5 rows stockinette stitch and cast off.

5. Join the edges of the neck trim and sew in the ends.

Unisex hoody

This hoody is a "cuddle up" cozy affair, ideal for wearing outside for summer cook-outs when the temperature drops. The textural edging gives it a special quality and updates the standard rib border with a 4 x 4 rib that is alternated into a chunky basketweave over 12 rows. One of the rewards of chunky knitting is that it grows fast! If you'd rather not do the basketweave, substitute a plain 4 x 4 rib to cover these 12 rows. You can go quite wild or be subtle and gentle with the colors on this one. If you use an individual design based on your three favorite colors, no one else will ever turn up in the same hoody!

EQUIPMENT

1 pair #10$^1/_2$ needles
1 circular #10$^1/_2$ needle (for hood)
2 x stitch holders
A row counter (optional)

YARN

Yarn A: Debbie Bliss Merino Chunky, shade 612 Dark Plum
Yarn B: Debbie Bliss Merino Chunky, shade 205 Teal
Yarn C: Debbie Bliss Merino Chunky, shade 700 Scarlet
Most chunky yarns that knit to this tension can be substituted.

SIZES

Small sizes are given in the instructions with medium, large and Xlarge in brackets.

	SMALL 6–8	MEDIUM 10–12	LARGE 14–16	XLARGE 16–18
Bust:	32–34in	36–38in	40–42$^1/_2$in	43–45in
	(81–86cm)	(91–97cm)	(102–108cm)	(110–115cm)
Finished bust	37$^3/_4$in	42$^1/_2$in	44$^3/_4$in	47in
	(96cm)	(108cm)	(114cm)	(120cm)
Finished length:	23in	23$^1/_2$in	24$^1/_2$in	25in
	(58cm)	(60cm)	(62cm)	(64cm)

YARN

(number of 50g balls)

	SMALL 6-8	MEDIUM 10-12	LARGE 14-16	XLARGE 16-18
A Main:	12	13	14	15
B Contrast:	8	9	9	10
C Stripe:	1	1	1	1

TENSION

Using #10$\frac{1}{2}$ needles with stockinette stitch 14 sts x 19 rows = 4in (10cm) square.

METHOD

Back

In yarn B on straight needles cast on 68 [76/80/84] sts.

Next row: K1 row.

Next row: Change to yarn A. *K4, P4 and rep from * until 4 sts from end, K4.

(Note: in the large size, there will not be the odd 4 sts to k or p at the end, and consequently the following row will read "K4, P4 to end").

Next row: *P4, K4, rep from * until 4 sts from end, P4.

Rep these previous 2 rows so there are 4 rows in total. You have now finished your first basketweave square.

Next row: *P4, K4, rep from * until 4 sts from end, P4.

(Note: in the large size, there will not be the odd 4 sts to K or P at the end, and consequently the following row will read "P4, K4 to end").

Next row: *K4, P4 rep from * until 4 sts from end, K4.

Rep these 2 rows so there are 4 rows in total. You have now finished your second basketweave square.

Rep the first basketweave square once more.

Next row: K1 row.

Starting with a knit row, work until your knitting measures 8$\frac{1}{2}$in [9/9$\frac{1}{2}$/10in] (22cm [23/24/25cm]) from the bottom edge. Make sure you end with a purl row.

Change to yarn C.

K2 rows.

Change to yarn B.

Work 20 rows in stockinette stitch (starting with a knit row).

Change to yarn C.

K2 rows.

Change to yarn A.

Work 2 rows stockinette stitch.

This brings you to the armhole shaping, which goes as follows:

Working in stockinette stitch, cast off 4 [3/4/4] sts at beginning of next 2 rows.

Work 8 rows, decreasing 1 stitch at each end of the knit rows. (If you can do this 1 stitch in from the edge, it makes sewing up easier and neater.) See method at end.

After the last purl row there should be 52 [62/64/68] sts left on needle.

Work in stockinette stitch until your knitting measures 8$\frac{1}{4}$in [9/9$\frac{1}{4}$/9$\frac{1}{2}$in] (21cm [23/23.5/24cm]) from the underarm cast off. Make sure you end with a knit row.

The shoulder and neck shaping (first side) goes as follows:

Next row: P21 [26/27/29] sts, place remaining 31 [36/37/39] sts on a stitch holder (these will be the back neck and the other shoulder).

Next row: Cast off 7 [7/8/8] sts (this is on the neck edge) at beginning of row, K to end.

Next row: Cast off 6 [7/7/7] sts at beginning of the row, P to end.

Next row: K1 row.

Next row: Cast off 5 [6/8/8] sts, P to end.

Final row: Cast off remaining sts and break yarn.

The shoulder and neck shaping (second side) goes as follows:

Take 21 [26/28/29] sts at the edge of the knitting off the stitch holder on to a needle, leaving the middle 10 on the holder and knit the left-hand shoulder.

Start with the wrong (purl) side facing you (you may need to shuffle sts from needle to needle to do this, but it makes it easier to knit).

Take a new end of yarn.

Row 1: P1 row.

Next row: Cast off 7 [7/7/8] sts at beginning of row, K to end.

Next row: Cast off 6 [7/8/8] sts at beginning of row, this is on the neck edge, P to end.

Next row: Cast off 5 [6/8/8] sts, K to end.

Final row: Cast off remaining sts, break yarn.

Leave middle sts on a stitch holder until the hood is knitted.

Front

Knit as the back until after the armhole shaping when there are 52 [62/66/68] sts left on the needle and your knitting measures 5³/₄in [6/6¹/₄/6¹/₂in] (14.5cm [15.5/16/16.5cm]) from the underarm cast off. Make sure you end with a knit row.

For the first neck shaping:

Next row: P21 [26/28/29] sts and place remaining 31 [36/38/39] sts on to a stitch holder.

Next row: Cast off 3 [4/4/5] sts at beginning of the row (this should be on the neck edge K to end).

Next row: P1 row

Next row: Cast off 2 [2/2/2] sts at beginning of the row, K to end.

Next row: P1 row.

Work straight stockinette stitch for 6 rows.

Next row: Decrease 1 [1/1/1] st at beginning of row and K to end.

The shoulder shaping comes in at the outside edge:

Next row: Cast off 6 [7/7/8] sts at beginning of row, P to end.

Next row: K1 row.

Next row: Cast off 5 [6/8/8] sts at beginning of row, P to end.

Next row: K1 row.

Row 1: Cast off remaining sts and break yarn.

For second neck shaping:

Take 21 [26/28/29] sts at the edge of the knitting off the holder on to a needle, leaving the middle 10 on the holder. Start with the wrong (purl) side facing you.

Take a new end of yarn.

Row 1: P1 row.

Next row: K1 row.

Next row: Cast off 3 [4/4/5] sts at beginning of row (this should be on the neck edge) K to end.

Next row: P1 row.

Next row: Cast off 2 [2/2/2] sts at beginning of row, K to end.

Next row: P1 row.

Work straight stockinette stitch for 6 rows.

Next row: Decrease 1 [1/1/1] st at beginning of row and K to end.

Now the shoulder shaping comes in at the outside edge:

Next row: Cast off 6 [7/7/8] sts at beginning of row, P to end.

Next row: K1 row.

Next row: Cast off 5 [6/8/8] sts at beginning of row, P to end.

Next row: K1 row.

Final row: Cast off remaining sts and break yarn.

Sleeves (both worked the same)

In yarn B on straight needles cast on 36 [36/38/38] sts.

Row 1: K1 row.

Change to yarn A.

Knit same pattern as for basketweave as on back, increasing 1 st each end on rows 4, 8 and 12. (For the two larger sizes, if you want the basketweave to match at the seams, you will need to start the pattern with P1 and then continue the *K4, P4* rep to the end where there will be K4, P2 to finish.)

K1 row.

Starting with a knit row, knit in stockinette stitch, increasing 1 st each end of the 2nd [7th/0th/4th] row and every following 5th [5th/6th/5th] row until your knitting measures 13³/₄in [14³/₄/15¹/₄/15³/₄in] (35cm [37.5/39/40cm]) from cast on. Make sure you end with a purl row.

Throughout the following rows, continue increasing on every 5th [5th/6th/5th] row as before.

Change to yarn C.

K2 rows.

Change to yarn B.

K20 rows in stockinette stitch. Stop increasing when there are 70 [72/74/76] sts on the needle.
Change to yarn C.
K2 rows.
Change to yarn A.
Work 2 rows in stockinette stitch (starting with a K row).

Start the underarm shaping:
Next 2 rows: Cast off 4 sts at beginning of both.
Next 24 [24/26/26] rows, decrease 1 st at both ends of every knit row only.
Next 4 rows: Cast off 3 [4/4/5] sts at beginning of each row.
Next 2 rows: Cast off 5 [5/5/5] sts at beginning of each row.
Final row: Mark center of remaining stitches and cast them off.

Hood
Sew up the shoulder seams.
In yarn A, with the circular needle, pick up 68 [72/78/82] sts evenly around the neck. Put a marker at the center front.
Knit 2 rows completely round in a circle.
Next row: K4 [6/9/11] sts, inc 1st, *K6, inc 1st*, rep * to * until last 4 [6/9/11] sts, knit to end.

Change to yarn B.
Next 4 rows: continue to knit in a circle, purling the 12 stitches at the center front, so they are in reverse stockinette stitch.
Next row: Turn the knitting and work back around the circle so there is a split at the center front. Carry on with the reverse stockinette stitch on the middle stitches as before.
Continue this, keeping the split in the center front for 78 [78/80/80] rows or until the knitting measures $15^5/_4$in [$15^5/_4$/16/16in] (40cm [40/41/41cm]) from neck edge.
Transfer the stitches equally to 2 needles, so the front of the hood is at the point of the needles and the right sides are facing.
Take a 3rd needle of roughly the same size.
To get a nice smooth join, cast off with the "three-needle cast-off", as follows:
Put both filled needles together and hold exactly as you would normally hold the left-hand needle.

Take the 3rd needle in your right hand and insert it through the 1st stitch on both needles in a knitwise manner.
Knit both stitches together.
Do the same again and then pull the 1st stitch you just made over the last one, as you would when casting off normally.
Carry on to the end repeating this process, and pulling the last stitch through.

Depending on your yarn, dry or wet block the pieces and sew up the side seams.

To decrease one stitch in from the edge at the beginning of a row gives a right-hand pointing slant to the stitch and is called the K2tog method:
On a knit row, K1 st, knit 2 together, K to end.
On a purl row, p1 st, purl 2 together and P to end.

To decrease one stitch in from the edge at the end of a row gives a left-hand pointing slant to the stitch and is called the Ssk or Slip, Slip, Knit method:
On a knit row, K to 3 sts from the end. Slip the next 2 sts one after the other knitwise off the left-hand needle. Then insert the left-hand needle up through the front of these sts from left to right. Bring your yarn through as usual and make a knit stitch.
On a purl row (Ssp or Slip, Slip, Purl) it is a little more complicated, so K to position and do the slipping as for a knit row, but then slip them back on to the left-hand needle and insert the right needle at the back up from below through both these stitches and purl them together.

Alpaca cardigan

This cardigan was inspired by the geometric filet-lace edgings often found on antique tablecloths. The moss stitch is knitted as you go along, creating a firm front border while also maintaining the garment's shape at the hip. The luxurious Alpaca Silk yarn (80 per cent Alpaca and 20 per cent silk) turns a simple cardigan into an exquisite, sensual experience. Accentuate this sensuous luxury by choosing a wide, softly flowing tonal ribbon as a decorative front fastening.

EQUIPMENT

1 pair #7 needles.
Stitch holder
Row counter (optional)

YARN

Debbie Bliss Alpaca Silk, shade 25010 Coral

RIBBON

2yds (2m) of 1¹/₂in (4cm) wide soft satin ribbon in a tone of the main color.

SIZES

Small sizes are given in the instructions with medium, large and Xlarge in brackets.

	SMALL 6–8	MEDIUM 10–12	LARGE 14–16	XLARGE 16–18
Bust:	32–34in	36–38in	40–42¹/₂in	43–45in
	(81–86cm)	91–97cm)	(102–108cm)	(110–115cm)
Finished bust:	36in	42¹/₂in	44³/₄in	47in
	(92cm)	(108cm)	(114cm)	(120cm)
Finished length:	22in	23¹/₂in	24¹/₂in	25in
	(56cm)	(60cm)	(62cm)	(64cm)

YARN

(number of 50g balls)

SMALL 6–8	MEDIUM 10–12	LARGE 14–16	XLARGE 16–18
13	16	19	21

TENSION

Using #7 needles with stockinette stitch 18 sts x 23 rows = 4in (10cm) square.

METHOD

Note: If you can do your shaping at the sides of the pieces one stitch in from the edge, it will give a prettier finish and a neater edge to sew up. The shaping at the front neck edge is already positioned inside the moss stitch in the pattern.

Back

If you want to do a decorative decrease, use Ssk (see page 57) on beginning the decrease and K2tog on the end one.

Cast on 82 [96/104/110] sts.
Work moss stitch border as follows:
K1, P1, rep * to * to end.
P1, K1, rep * to * to end.
Repeat these 2 rows until there are 8 rows of knitting.

Work 2 rows stockinette stitch, decreasing 1st each end on the 2nd row.
Work 20 rows of the main pattern, decreasing 1st each end every 10th row.
Work 10 rows of the main pattern increasing 1st each end on the 10th row.
In stockinette stitch, carry on as follows:
Work 32 [36/38/42] rows, increasing 1st each end every 13 [16/17/18] rows.

Start of underarm shaping:

Cast off 3 [4/5/5] sts at beginning of next 2 rows.

Work 1 [1/3/6] rows, decreasing 1st each end.

Work 14 [16/16/12] rows, decreasing 1st at each underarm edge on every 2nd row.

Next row: Work straight in stockinette stitch to row 116 [126/130/134] or until knitting measures 20in [22^1/$_2$/22^1/$_2$/23in] (51cm [57/57.5/58.5cm]) from cast-on edge.

Start of neck and shoulder shaping:

In this shaping the cast-offs are given a smoother line (instead of the traditional "steps") by knitting 2 sts together at the end of the preceding row. This tip is borrowed from Elizabeth Zimmerman's *Knitting Without Tears*. It is described here, and it could also be applied to the front-panel shoulder shaping.

Next row: K27 [28/29/30] sts, put remaining sts on a holder, putting in a center-back marker at middle of whole piece.

Next row: Turn knitting and cast off 4 [4/4/5] sts at neck edge, P to end.

Next row: K to end, knitting last 2 sts together.

Next row: Cast off 2 [3/4/3] sts at neck edge, P to end.

Next row: Cast off 4 [3/3/4] sts at shoulder edge and K to end, knitting last 2 sts together at neck edge.

Next row: Cast off 1 [0/0/0] sts at neck edge, P to end of row, purling last 2 sts together at shoulder edge.

Next row: Cast off 3 [3/4/3] sts at shoulder edge and K to end, knitting last 2 sts together at neck edge.

Next row: P to end, purling last 2 sts together at shoulder edge.

Next row: Cast off 4 [3/3/3] sts at shoulder edge and K to end.

Next row: P to end, purling last 2 sts together at shoulder edge.

Next row: Cast off remaining sts.

Front

Pattern A:

This is the basic pattern with the moss stitch integrated into the front panel.

*K to 4 sts from end, K1, P1, K1, P1.

P1, K1, P1, K1, P to end*. Rep * to *.

If you want to do decorative decreasing, it is worked as follows for the shaping on the sides of the body:

On a knit row: K1, decrease 1 st using Ssk method (see page 51), K to 4 sts from edge, K1, P1, K1, P1.

On a purl row: P1, K1, P1, K1, P to 3 sts from the edge and decrease 1 st by Ssp method (see page 51).

Decrease B:

The decreasing for the V-neck worked inside the moss stitch is as follows:

On a knit row: K to 6 stitches from end, decrease 1 stitch (K2tog), K1, P1, K1, P1.

On a purl row: P1, K1, P1, K1, decrease 1st (P2tog), P to end.

Left-hand side:
Cast on 40 [48/52/54] sts and knit moss stitch as back for 8 rows:
Row 1: *K1, P1*, rep * to *.
Next row: *P1, K1*, rep * to *.

Work 2 rows main pattern, decreasing 1st at the side edge on row 2.
Work 20 [20/24/20] rows of the main pattern, decreasing 1st at the side edge every 10 [10/8/10] rows.
Work 10 [10/6/10] rows of the main pattern, increasing 1st at the side edge at row 10 [10/6/10].

Start of front V shaping:
Next row: Work 1 row as decrease B (this will be a decrease on the front edge, inside the moss stitch border).
Work 18 [18/38/42] rows of the main pattern decreasing as decrease B, inside the moss stitch every 6 [6/7/6] rows, and increasing on the side edge every 9 [15/11/17] rows.
Note: For large size only, knit 3 rows straight and skip the next instruction, going straight to the underarm shaping.

Work 14 [18/0/0] rows of the main pattern decreasing as decrease B, inside the moss stitch every 6 [7/0/0] rows, and increasing on the side edge every 9 [15/0/0] rows.

Start of underarm shaping:
Continue with the front decreases at every 7 [7/7/6] rows to the end of the panel, but cast off 3 [3/5/5] sts on the side edge for the underarm on the next knit row.
Work 1 [1/3/6] rows, decreasing 1st every other row at the underarm edge.
Work 14 [16/18/12] rows, decreasing 1st at the underarm edge on every 2nd row.
Next row: Continuing the front decreasing, knit straight up on the armhole side edge for 34 [36/36/38] rows. This will bring you to the shoulder.

Start the shoulder shaping:
Still working in main pattern A, cast off 4 [4/4/5] sts on the shoulder edge on the next knit row.

Next row: P1 row pattern A.
Next row: Cast off 4 [5/5/5] sts on the shoulder edge.
Next row: P1 row pattern A.
Next row: Cast off 5 [5/5/5] sts on the shoulder edge.
Next row: P1 row pattern A.
Next row: Cast off remaining sts.
Right-hand side:
Pattern A:
This is the basic pattern with the moss stitch integrated into the front panel.
*K to 4 sts from end, K1, P1, K1, P1.
P1, K1, P1, K1, P to end*. Rep * to *.

If you want to do decorative decreasing, it is worked as follows for the shaping on the sides of the body:
On a knit row: P1, K1, P1, K1, K to 3 sts from end, decrease 1 stitch (K2tog).
On a purl row: P1, decrease 1st (P2tog), P to 4 sts from end, K1, P1, K1, P1.

Decrease B:
The decreasing for the V-neck worked inside the moss stitch is as follows:
On a knit row: P1, K1, P1, K1, decrease 1st (Ssk, see page 57), K to end.
On a purl row: P to 6 sts from end, decrease 1 stitch (Ssp, see page 57), K1, P1, K1, P1.

Right-hand side:
Cast on 40 [48/52/54] and knit moss stitch as back for 8 rows:
Row 1: *K1, P1*, rep * to *.
Next row: *P1, K1*, rep * to *.

Work 2 [2/2/2] rows main pattern, decreasing 1st at the side edge every 2 [2/2/2] rows.
Work 20 [20/24/20] rows of the main pattern, decreasing 1st at the side edge every 10 [10/8/10] rows.
Work 10 [10/6/10] rows of the main pattern, increasing 1st at the side edge at row 10 [10/6/10].

Start of front V shaping:

Next row: Work 1 row as decrease B (this will be a decrease on the front edge, inside the moss-stitch border).

Work 18 [18/38/42] rows of the main pattern decreasing as decrease B, inside the moss stitch every 6 [6/7/6] rows, and increasing on the side edge every 9 [15/11/17] rows.

Note: For large size only, knit 3 rows straight and skip the next instruction, going straight to the underarm shaping.

Work 14 [18/0/0] rows of the main pattern decreasing as decrease B, inside the moss stitch every 6 [7/0/0] rows, and increasing on the side edge every 9 [15/0/0] rows.

Start of underarm shaping:

Continue with the front decreases at every 7 [7/7/6] rows to the end of the panel, but cast off 3 [3/5/5] sts on the side edge for the underarm on the next knit row.

Work 1 [1/3/6] rows, decreasing 1st every other row at the underarm edge.

Work 14 [16/18/12] rows, decreasing 1st at the underarm edge on every 2nd row.

Next row: Continuing the front decreasing, knit straight up on the armhole side edge for 34 [36/36/38] rows. This will bring you to the shoulder.

Start the shoulder shaping:

Working in main pattern A, cast off 4 [4/4/5] sts on the shoulder edge on the next knit row.

Next row: P1 row pattern A.

Next row: Cast off 4 [5/5/5] sts on the shoulder edge.

Next row: P1 row pattern A.

Next row: Cast off 5 [5/5/5] sts on the shoulder edge.

Next row: P1 row pattern A.

Next row: Cast off remaining sts.

Sleeves

(Both are the same.)

Cast on 42 [46/48/50] sts and knit moss stitch as for back. Continue in stockinette stitch as follows starting with a K row:

Next row: Increase 1st at each end of row.

Next section: Work 91 [93/30/72] rows in stockinette stitch, increasing 1st at each edge every 8 [7/6/6] rows.

Next section: Work 0 [0/63/23] rows in stockinette stitch, increasing 1st at each edge every 0 [0/7/7] rows until your work measures 17in [18/18/18in] (43.5cm [45/45/45cm]) from the cast-on edge. Finish on a P row.

Next row: Cast off 4 [3/3/4] sts at beginning of row, K to end.

Next row: Cast off 4 [3/3/4] sts at beginning of row, P to end.

Next row: Work 4 [7/8/7] rows stockinette stitch, decreasing 1st at each end of every row.

Next row: Work 6 [9/12/4] rows stockinette stitch, decreasing 1st at each end of every 3 [3/3/4] rows.

Next row: Work 18 [12/10/7] rows stockinette stitch, decreasing 1st at each end of every 2 [2/2/3] rows.

Next row: Work 1 [7/7/7] rows stockinette stitch, decreasing 1st each at end of every 1 [1/1/1] rows.

Next row: Cast off remaining sts marking center of sleeve head. 20 [22/24/26]. Row 134 [138/140/142].

Making up

1. Block out carefully as the moss stitch has a tendency to curl – in fact, the whole garment will benefit from this. To make everything easier while sewing up, line up the decreases as you do this.

2. Do all the sewing in the yarn in which the garment is knitted. Join the shoulder seams, matching moss stitch patterns and preferably using mattress stitch (see page 41).

3. Set in the sleeves, matching the center sleeve head to the shoulder seam and easing in any fullness. Sew up with mattress stitch.

4. Join the side seams and the underarm seams with mattress stitch. Take care to match up the decreases to give a professional finish.

5. Finally, sew in ends and sew on the ribbons, positioning them at the bottom of the front decreases.

Fingerless gloves

These cute and cozy gloves have a little pocket on the front and are very simple to make. If you can cast on and off, rib and do simple increases, you will have no problems knitting these.

EQUIPMENT
1 pair #7 needles
1 pair #8 needles

YARN
Yarn A: 1 x 50g ball Debbie Bliss Cashmerino Aran, shade 502 Pea Green
Yarn B: 1 x 50g ball Debbie Bliss Cashmerino Aran, shade 505 Yellow
Yarn C: 1 x 50g ball Debbie Bliss Cashmerino Aran, shade 609 Burnt Orange

TENSION
Using #8 needles 18sts x 24 rows = 4in (10cm) square.

METHOD
With the #7 needles and yarn B, cast on 36 stitches using the two-strand thumb method by preference, but any method will do.

The two-strand thumb method
This technique that uses the thumb as another needle makes a firm but elastic cast on that's good for rib edges.
Leaving a tail of yarn 3 times as long as the proposed wrist circumference, cast on, make a slip knot, and slip it over the right-hand needle.
1. Hold the needle in your right hand and the tail of yarn in your left hand, so it is gripped underneath your turned-under fingers, leaving a strand of approximately 4in (10cm) stretching from your left hand towards the right-hand needle.
2. Lay your thumb over the top of this strand and draw an counter-clockwise circle with the end of your thumb so

the yarn is wrapped clockwise neatly around it.
3. Next slide the tip of the right-hand needle up under the front loop on your thumb, and pass the right-hand yarn over from the back between thumb and needle, as if making a knit stitch.
4. Slip the loop off your left thumb as if completing the knit stitch; pull the tails to tighten the stitch and repeat for as many stitches as you need to cast on.

While knitting these gloves, keep checking the size against your hand; if they need adjusting in length, do half the extra rows in the plain section after the increasing for the thumb and the rest in the straight section after the thumb hole.

Right-hand glove
Work 18 rows in K1, P1 rib to create the wrist rib.
Change to #8 needles and yarn A.
Work 2 rows stockinette stitch.
**Then continue in stockinette stitch as follows: *increase 1 st on third-from-last st at the end of the next row by knitting into front and back* (see increase instructions on page 29), (37 sts on needle).
P1 row*.
Rept * to * until there are 42 sts on the needle.
You've now finished the right thumb shaping.
Work 14 rows in stockinette stitch.

Creating the thumb hole:
Cast off 14 sts at the end of the row and cut your yarn, leaving a tail.
On the empty needle, with new yarn, cast on 10 sts, bring the yarn to the front, and continue to purl the stitches on the other needle, knitting the tail with the new yarn for a few stitches to catch it in (38 sts on needle).**
Work 2 rows in stockinette stitch.
Change to yarn B.
Work 4 rows in stockinette stitch.
Change to #7 needles.

Work 4 rows in K1, P1 rib.

Cast off as normal on the knit stitches but where there is a purl stitch, take the yarn back when you slip the second stitch over the first stitch and bring it back again if you want to purl the next stitch.

Left–hand glove

Knit as right–hand glove, swapping the shaping instructions ** to ** to the opposite side and then continuing to the end as with the right glove.

Cast off.

The little pocket

Using #7 needles and yarn C, and starting from about the 6th stitch in from the thumb-hole edge, pick up 9 sts along the 10th row up from the end of the wrist rib.

(To do this, have the right side facing and one needle in your right hand, then push the needle from front to back through the center of the existing stitch. Wind the yarn around the needle in a knit action and draw the loop through to create a new stitch on the needle). When you finish this row, the yarn will be on the wrong side of the knitting, so break it and start with a fresh end. You can vary the position depending on the size of pocket you want.

Break your yarn (it is on the wrong side of the fabric).

K1 row into the back of the stitches.

P1 row.

Work another 8 rows in stockinette stitch.

Cast off.

Pocket flap

This has a bit of increasing and decreasing to shape the edges with a left and right slant. It's rather pretty, but if it's not your thing, just knit the flap straight for 6 rows, cast off and add a loop as described. You can try shaping another time!

Find the row that is 2 rows above the cast off of the pocket edge and using yarn A, pick up through 11 sts, as you did with the pocket, starting from 1 st outside the width of the

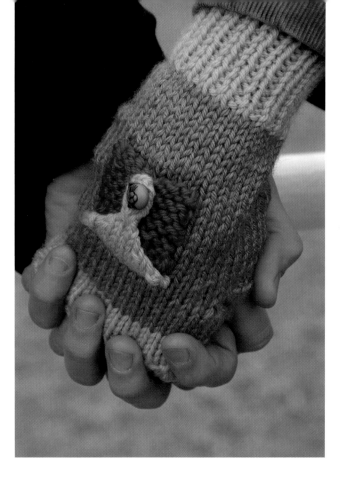

pocket and ending one st outside the other end.

K1 row into the back of the stitches.

P1 row.

Work another 6 rows stockinette stitch, decreasing 1 st each end until 3 sts are left on the needle.

If you use the Ssk method (see page 57) on the first decrease in the row it looks better. On a knit row, slip 1 knitwise twice, insert left needle into front of these 2 sts from the left and K2tog; on a purl row, slip one knitwise twice, return these 2 sts to left needle, insert right needle from back upwards through second.

Cast off.

With a crochet hook, chain a button loop on the pocket flap.

Sew up the thumb seam with mattress stitch, using the ends of the yarns where possible and matching the color to that of the stripe you are joining.

Sew in any odd ends.

Mark where the joins between the fingers occur and sew or crochet a chain across with yellow yarn.

Finally, add the button of your choice to the pocket flap.

Poncho

Although this poncho looks luxurious and weighty, it is in fact very light – and incredibly warm. The mixing of the different quality yarns adds visual texture. If you don't want to wear it as a poncho, why not just decadently wrap it around your neck and shoulders – and create a snug cocoon for yourself?

EQUIPMENT
1 pair #35 needles

YARN
3 x 100g balls Rowan Biggy Print, shade 237 Tickle
1 x 50g ball Rowan Handknit Cotton, shade 313 Slick

METHOD
Using the chunky (Rowan Biggy Print) yarn, cast on 20 sts. Knit 4 rows of stockinette stitch and break off the yarn.
Change to the finer Handknit Cotton yarn and knit 4 rows of stockinette stitch and break off the yarn.
Change to the chunky (Rowan Biggy Print) yarn and knit 4 rows of stockinette stitch.
Continue with these yarn stripes in blocks of 4 rows until you have 28 rows or 7 bands of chunky (Rowan Biggy Print) stripes.
Cast off.

Knit a second identical piece.

1 Join the 2 pieces together, leaving a central opening of approximately 10in (25cm) for the head.
2 To add the fringe, cut about 100 x 10in (25cm) lengths of Rowan Biggy Print yarn.
3 Place them around the edge of the poncho, deciding on the space intervals (2–2$\frac{1}{2}$in/5–6cm seems about right). Then attach the fringe.

Cotton summer hat

Using cotton for this item makes a comfortably soft but easily reshaped hat for the beach or any hot summer's day. You can pack it tightly in a bag or pocket, give it a quick shake and it's ready to go. Play your own color games and have fun with the stripes to match your wardrobe. Choose a bright and sassy version or a subtle and laid-back interpretation – it's up to you!

EQUIPMENT
1 pair #5 needles
Row counter (optional)

YARN
1 x 50g ball Rowan Handknit Cotton in each of the following 3 colors:
Yarn A: shade 318 Seafarer
Yarn B: shade 320 Buttercup
Yarn C: shade 319 Mango Fool

SIZING
A hat with a $21^1/_2$–23in (55–58cm) head circumference like this one should fit most head measurements.

TENSION
Using #5 needles with stockinette stitch 20 sts x 30 rows = 4in (10cm) square.

ABBREVIATIONS
yfwd (yarn forwards)
sl1 (slip 1)
ybk (yarn back)
Ssk or the Slip, Slip, Knit method (see also Unisex hoody on page 54): On a knit row, when you get to where the decrease is required, slip the next 2 sts one after the other knitwise off the left-hand needle on to the right hand one. Then insert the left-hand needle up through the front of these sts from left to right. Bring your yarn through as usual and make a knit stitch.

Ssp or the Slip, Slip, Purl method: On a purl row, when you get to where the decrease is required, slip the next 2 sts one after the other knitwise off the left-hand needle on to the right hand one. Then slip them back on to the left hand needle. Insert the right needle at the back upwards from below through both these stitches and purl them together.

METHOD
With yarn A, cast on 115 sts.
Work 8 rows stockinette stitch ending with a P row.
Change to yarn C, K2 rows garter stitch.
Change to yarn B, K8 rows stockinette stitch, starting with a K row.
Change to yarn A.
Work 30 rows in linen stitch as follows:
Row 1: *K1, yfwd, sl1 purlwise, ybk. Rep from * to last stitch, K1.
Row 2: P1, *P1, ybk, sl1 purlwise, yfwd. Rep from * to last 2 sts, P2.

The linen stitch reduces stretch in the band so it gently grips the head while adding textural interest.

K1 row, increasing 1st at end of the row.

Work 7 rows in stockinette stitch, increasing 1 st at each end of 1st row (118 sts).

Change to yarn B, work 7 rows stockinette stitch, ending with a P row.

Change to yarn C, work 5 rows in garter stitch. On the 6th row, at every 4th stitch before making the stitch, reach down with the needle tip and catch the top loop of the last stitch in yarn B that is directly below the current stitch and make the new stitch through both loops. This pulls the knitting into a ripple and makes the rim of the crown.

Change to yarn A and K1 row, putting markers after the 13th stitch and between the following 4 blocks of 23 stitches (there should be another 13 left at the end).

For the crown shaping:

Work from now on in stockinette stitch, starting with a P row.

Next row: *P1 row, decreasing 1st both sides of the markers. In each pair, 1st decrease should be P2tog, 2nd should be Ssp method (see above).

Next row: K1 row.

Next row: P1 row.

Next row: K1 row, decreasing 1st both sides of the markers. In each pair, 1st decrease should be Ssk method (see above), 2nd should be K2tog method.

Next row: P1 row.

Next row: K1 row, decreasing 1st both sides of the markers. In each pair, 1st decrease should be Ssk method (see above), 2nd should be K2tog method.

Next row: P1 row.

Next row: K1 row.

Next row: P1 row, decreasing 1st both sides of the markers. In each pair, 1st decrease should be P2tog, 2nd should be Ssp method (see above).

Next row: K1 row*.

Next 10 rows: Rep * to *.

Next row: P1 row.

Next row: K1 row, decreasing 1st both sides of the markers.

In each pair, 1st decrease should be Ssk method (see above), 2nd should be K2tog method.

Next 2 rows: P1 row.

Next row: K1 row, decreasing 1st both sides of the markers. In each pair, 1st decrease should be Ssk method (see above), 2nd should be K2tog method.

Next row: Thread yarn through the remaining 6 sts at the apex of the decreases.

Sew up the seam, matching yarn colors, draw last 6 sts into a point and sew in the ends securely.

Block over a tubular shape that will help the hat form a nice fit.

Dare-to-wear bikini

This funky bikini can compete confidently with the very latest beach fashions. The top could also be worn with shorts for a more sporty look. There is no doubt that this bikini is minimal and "dare to wear", so pull both elements tight to fit snugly! The bikini is available in two sizes, small and medium, with the small size given first and the medium size following in brackets.

EQUIPMENT
1 pair #6 needles
1 pair #3 needles

YARN
1 x 50g balls Rowan Handknit DK Cotton, shade 309 Celery (edging)
2 x 50g ball Rowan Handknit DK Cotton, shade 313 Slick (main color)
1 x 50g ball Rowan Handknit DK Cotton, shade 319 Mango Fool (flower)

TENSION
Using #6 needles 20 sts x 28 rows = 4in (10cm) square.

ABBREVIATIONS
K2tog (knit 2 stitches together)
K2tog tbl (knit 2 stitches together through back loop)

METHOD
Top
Row 1: Using #6 needles and the edging color, cast on 35 [39] sts.
Row 2: Change to main color.
Row 3: Knit 1 row into the back of the stitch.
Row 4: Purl 1 row.
Row 5: On the next row begin to knit the flower image after knitting 6 sts in the main color. Copy the pattern from the chart shown here, while following the shaping instructions given below.

Shaping 1: K15 [17], K2tog tbl, K1, K2tog, K15 [17].
Shaping 2: Purl 1 row.
Shaping 3: K14 [16], K2tog tbl, K1, K2tog, K14 [16].
Shaping 4: Purl 1 row.
Shaping 5: Continue in this way, decreasing by a single stitch the number of stitches worked before K2tog tbl, K1, K2tog, and decrease by a single stitch the number of stitches knitted to the end of the row.

Next row: Purl 1 row.
Next row: Continue following these last 2 rows until 3 sts remain.
Next row: Purl 1 row.
Next row: Change to #3 needles to knit cord for tie. Use main color. Knit 3.

Next row: Slip these 3 sts back to needle in left hand.

Next row: Knit 3.

Next row: Continue in this way until the cord reaches approx. 11$\frac{1}{2}$in (29cm). Cast off.

Next row: Now add the trim. This will neaten the edge and allow you to add a highlight color using #3 needles and the main color. With right side facing, pick up and knit up 1 side of top. Turn and knit back. Then cast off using the edging color.

Next row: Repeat up the other side.

Next row: Pick up 3 sts at center front of one side, knit in the same way as the cord for approximately 2$\frac{1}{2}$in (6cm). Cast off. Join to the other side's center front. You may want to adjust this distance depending on your individual chest measurements.

Next row: Pick up 3 sts at one side of top, knit in the same way as the cord for approximately 19$\frac{1}{2}$in (50cm). Cast off. Repeat on the other side.

Bottoms

Row 1: Using #6 needles and the edging color, cast on 28 [32] sts.

Change to main yarn.

Row 2: Knit 1 row into back of stitch.

Row 3: Purl 1 row.

Row 4: On the next row begin to knit the flower image after knitting 6 sts in the main color. Copy the pattern from the chart shown here, while following the shaping instructions given below.

Shaping 1: K2tog, knit to last 2 sts, K2tog.

Shaping 2: Purl.

Shaping 3: Continue in stockinette stitch, decreasing 2 sts (as in shaping 1) every 5 rows until 14 sts remain.

Shaping 4: Continue in stockinette stitch, decreasing 2 sts every 3 rows until 10 sts remain.

Shaping 5: Knit 4 rows.

Shaping 6: Increase 1 st, knit to last st, then increase 1 st.

Shaping 7: Continue in stockinette stitch, increasing 2 st every 4 rows (as in shaping 6) until you have 22 sts.

Shaping 8: Continue in stockinette stitch, increasing 2 sts every 3 rows until 50 [54] sts are on the needle.

Shaping 9: Using edging color cast off.

Next row: Using #3 needles, and with right side facing, pick up and knit around the leg edge of one side of the pants.

Next row: Knit.

Next row: Using edging color, cast off.

Next 3 rows: Repeat previous 3 rows on the other side.

Next row: Using #3 needles, and with right side facing, pick up and knit 3 sts at top the edge of the bottoms. Knit in the same way as the cord for approx. 12$\frac{1}{2}$in (32cm). Cast off.

Repeat the above sequence on the other top edges to form the ties for the bottoms.

Knit the flower image in intarsia (to avoid having any floats of yarn on the reverse).

Each color block has its own ball of yarn, so make little wrappings of the colors you will need. Knit in stockinette stitch, following the chart. When you change from one color to another, twist one yarn around the other to link the color blocks.

MOTIF

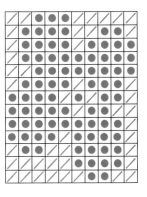

Cell phone/iPod cover

This funky cover for a cell phone, or for an iPod, is an ideal gift and a great excuse to show off your knitting skills. Use any combination of colors, and any double-knit yarn can be used for the main color. In the motif pattern, Aran has been used for the motif in order to make the pink heart stand out, but any yarn can be used. Alternatively, as with the sock-yarn pattern, try using self-patterning sock yarn. There's no fiddling around with changing colors – you just knit from one ball of wool and use the size needles recommended for the yarn.

EQUIPMENT
1 pair #8 needles (for motif cover)
1 pair #4 needles (for sock-yarn cover)
Lining
1 snap fastener
1 button

YARN
Motif cover
Yarn A: 1 x 50g ball Rowan Wool Cotton, shade 946 Elf
Yarn B: 1 x 50g ball Debbie Bliss Cashmerino Aran, shade 616 Fuchsia

Sock-yarn cover
1 x 50g ball 6-ply Regia Sock Yarn, shade 5269 Las Vegas

TENSION
Using #8 needles 22 sts x 24 rows = 4in (10cm) square (Wool Cotton).
Using #4 needles 26 sts x 32 rows = 4in (10cm) square (Sock Yarn).

METHOD
Work in stockinette stitch throughout (K x 1 row, P x 1 row).

Motif cover
1. Cast on 21 sts in yarn A.
2. Work 18 rows ending on a purl row.
3. Follow motif chart (A) using yarn A and B for next 13 rows, using the Fairisle technique (see page 34).
4. Work 20 rows in yarn A.
5. Follow motif chart (B) using yarn A and B for next 13 rows.
6. Work 22 rows in yarn A, ending with a purl row.
7. Decrease 1 st at each end of the next knit row and every following knit row until 11 sts remain.
8. Purl 1 row.
9. Cast off.

Sock-yarn cover
1. Cast on 21 sts in yarn A.
2. Work 86 rows in stockinette stitch, ending with a purl row.
3. Decrease 1 st at each end of the next knit row and every following knit row until 11 sts remain.
4. Purl 1 row.
5. Cast off.

Making up

Sew in ends.

Block and press.

Lining and finishing

1. Lay the knitted piece flat and measure a piece of lining fabric ¹/₃in (1cm) bigger than the knitted piece to allow for the seam. Lay the front face of the lining to the front face of the knitted piece and machine-sew 3 sides, leaving the top open. When you are stitching, leave the edges of the knitted stitches free so the sides can be sewn up later.

2. Turn the fabric inside out to reveal the right side of the knitted piece. At the top edge tuck the lining edge under and hand-stitch the rest of the lining to the knitted piece.

3. Fold so the right side is facing the right side and then bring the bottom edge of the fabric up to ¹/₃in (1cm) below the point where the decreasing starts and stitch the two side seams with the over-and-over method. Press the seams.

4. Sew a snap fastener on the inside of the flap and sew on a button as a decoration.

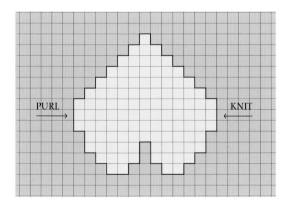

PURL →   KNIT ←

Chart A

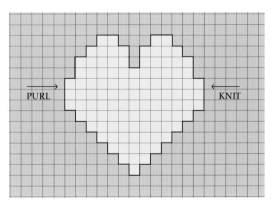

PURL →   KNIT ←

Chart B

Leg warmers

There is no need for leg warmers to be associated solely with the sporting and street fashions of the 1980s – they are now officially back on the streets in confident contemporary styles. This design, using a Cashmerino mix with Merino wool, provides the perfect comfort clothing for those cold winter days. This pattern can be used in combination with any chunky yarn.

EQUIPMENT
1 pair #10^1/$_2$ needles

YARN
2 x 100g balls Debbie Bliss Cashmerino Superchunky, shade 11 Red

TENSION
Using #10^1/$_2$ needles 12 sts x 17 rows = 4in (10cm) square.

METHOD
Knit both leg warmers in the same way.

Cast on 34 sts using #10^1/$_2$ needles.

Knit a 2-stitch rib as follows:
Row 1: K2 *P2, K2 rep from * to end.
Row 2: P2, *K2, P2, rep from * to end.

Continue these two rows until work measures 12in (30.5cm). Cast off in rib, making sure you take the yarn back when knitting and the yarn forward when purling your stitches.

Making up
Press each knitted piece (see page 42).
Sew up the seams.

Throw

This throw has an impressive selection of textures. The yarns have been chosen for their softness, so say goodbye to those annoying itchy blankets when you're curled up on the sofa. The throw is knitted in one piece, and on circular needles to hold the large amount of stitches. A neutral colorway has been chosen for this throw, but choose a color combination that matches your own décor.

EQUIPMENT
1 pair circular #10 needles 39¹/₄in (100cm) long
Stitch holder

YARN
Yarn A: 2 x 100g balls Rowan Ribbon Twist, shade 116 Riches

Yarn B: 4 x 50g balls Rowan Handknit Cotton, shade 253 Tope

Yarn C: 2 x 100g balls Rowan Polar, shade 645 Winter White

Yarn D: 2 x 50g balls Rowan Cotton Glacé, shade 730 Oyster (knit in a double thickness in combination with the Lurex Shimmer)

Yarn E: 1 x 25g ball Rowan Lurex Shimmer, shade 332 Antique White Gold (knit in a double thickness in combination with the Cotton Glacé)

Yarn F: 1 x 25g ball Rowan Lurex Shimmer, shade 330 Copper (knit in a double thickness in combination with the Cotton Glacé)

Yarn G: 3 x 100g skeins Debbie Bliss Maya, shade 07/062 (1¹/₂ ball for the main throw and 1¹/₂ ball for the edging)

Yarn H: 2 x 50g balls Debbie Bliss Alpaca Silk, shade 02 Cream

Yarn I: 1 x 100g skein Colinette Silkychic Tapis

METHOD
*Using a color and yarn of your choice, knit 6 rows in garter stitch (knit).
Change color and yarn. Knit 6 rows in stockinette stitch (K1 row, P1 row)*.

Continue from * to * until throw measures 48in (122.5cm) or the required length.
Cast off.

For the edging:
Owing to the throw having a mixture of textures and yarn thicknesses, the edges will have an uneven quality. The throw will therefore be held together better with an edging.

1. Cast on 9 sts in yarn G.
2. Rows 1-2: *K1, P1* repeat *to* to end of row. This sets moss stitch. Repeat until work measures 200in (5.1m) or is at the required length.
3. Put the stitches on a stitch holder until you are certain that the edging is long enough for the throw, then cast off.
4. Sew the edging on the throw using the over-and-over method (see page 40).
5. Fold the edging to go round the corners of the throw. Then stitch the corners in place.

Tasseled garter stitch scarf and Garter stitch scarf

A scarf in garter stitch, the simplest of knitting structures using just knit stitch, is an ideal first project for beginners, particularly when in combination with chunky yarn and chunky needles. To give a touch of glamor, add some tassels to decorate the sides of the scarf. Any superchunky yarn can be used for this pattern, so choose your preferred yarn and color and just start knitting.

EQUIPMENT
1 pair #17 needles (with Colinette Point Five yarn)
1 pair #19 needles (with Rowan Biggy Print yarn)

YARN
3 x 100g hanks Colinette Point Five, Blue Parrot
or
3 x 100g balls Rowan Biggy Print, shade 257 Choc Chip

TENSION
Colinette Point Five yarn: using #17 needles 8 sts x 10 rows = 4in (10cm) square.
Rowan Biggy Print yarn: using #19 needles 7.5 sts x 11.5 rows = 4in (10cm) square.

FINISHED SIZE
Length with Colinette Point Five yarn: 67in (171cm).
Length with Rowan Biggy Print yarn: 63$^{1}/_{2}$in (162cm).

TASSELLED SCARF

(using Point Five yarn)

With #17 needles, cast on 12 sts.
Sl st, K to end.
Repeat * to * until 2 skeins of yarn have been knitted, leaving enough yarn to cast off.
Sew in ends.

To make the tassels, wrap the yarn twice around your hand or a piece of card measuring approximately 3in (8.5cm) – this makes a 4-strand tassel.
Attach the tassels on every other row along the bottom and side ends (see fringe instructions on page 46).

GARTER STITCH SCARF

(using Rowan Biggy Print yarn)

With #19 needles, cast on 8 sts.
Sl st, K to end.
Repeat * to * until all 3 balls of yarn are used up, leaving just enough yarn to cast off.
Sew in ends.

Tip: use a crochet hook to sew in the ends of superchunky yarns. Alternatively, use a wool sewing needle with a large enough eye to thread superthick yarn.

Fluffy silky-chic scarf

This glamorous scarf wraps around the neck and ties at the front. The eyelash yarn is soft and silky and feels very luxurious.

EQUIPMENT
1 pair #10 needles
Approximately 12 beads

YARN
1 x 100g skein Colinette Silkychic, shade Toscana

TENSION
Using #10 needles 18 sts x 24 rows = 4in (10cm) square.

METHOD
Work in garter stitch (knit) throughout.

Cast on 1 st, leaving a 5in (13.5cm) tail.
Row 1: K1.
Row 2: Increase 1 st (2 sts).
Row 3: K2.
Row 4: Increase 1 st, inc 1 st (4 sts).
Row 5: Knit to end.
Row 6: Increase 1 st, knit to last st, inc 1 st (6 sts).

Repeat rows 5 and 6 until 16 sts remain on needle.
Knit straight until work measures 67in (1.7m).

Next row: K2tog, K to last st, K2tog.
Next row: Knit.
Repeat last 2 rows until 1 st remains.
Cast off, leaving a 8in (20cm) tail.

Make 2 tassels (see page 46), thread the tail with beads and stitch 1 tassel at each end of the scarf.

Beanie hat

All in all, this is just one evening's work. So, if the temperature drops, get home, dig out some fat needles and chunky yarn and by the morning you'll have made a warm hat – and an enviable fashion statement.

EQUIPMENT
1 pair #15 needles

YARN
1 x 100g ball Rowan Big Wool, shade 001 White Hot (also shown in shade 014 Whoosh)

TENSION
Using size #15 needles 8.5 sts x 13 rows = 4in (10cm) square.

METHOD
Knit in stockinette stitch throughout.
Small size in first parentheses, large size in brackets.

Cast on 37 [45] sts.
Knit 18 [20] rows in stockinette stitch.

Shaping the top:
Tip: Be sure to count the stitches at the end of each row when shaping.

Next row 1: With rs facing *K9, K2tog, rep from * to last st, K1 (33 [41] sts).
Next row 2: Work 1 row.
Next row 3: *K7, K3tog, rep from * to end (25 [33] sts).
Next row 4: Work 1 row.
Next row 5: *K5, K3tog, rep from * to end (17 [25] sts).
Next row 6: Work 1 row.

Small size only:
Next row 7: *K2, K2tog, rep from * to end (13 sts).

Next row 8: *P1, P2tog, rep from * to end (9 sts).

Large size only:
Next row 7: *K3, K3tog, rep from * to end (17 [17] sts).
Next row 8: *P1, P2tog, rep from * to end (11 [11] sts).
Next row 9: K3, K2tog, K3, K2tog, K1 (9 sts).
Next row 10: Work 1 row.

Both sizes:
Break the yarn, leaving a long tail. Thread the yarn through the remaining stitches. Pull up tight to create the crown and use the remaining yarn to sew up the hat.

Making up
Press as described on page 42.

Beaded make-up bag

This is the height of luxury in make-up bags. If you pull this out to find your lipstick, there's no doubt you'll look like a million dollars. Lined in velvet, it could also double up as a jewelry bag. It makes the perfect gift for someone special, particularly if you fill it with make-up, candy, soaps, or even jewels. The Cashmerino yarn makes it incredibly soft, but you can knit with any Aran-weight yarn.

EQUIPMENT

1 pair #9 needles
362 beads
Lining
1 snap faster
1 knitted flower (see page 47 for instructions)

YARN

1 x 50g ball Debbie Bliss Cashmerino Aran, shade 603 Pink

TENSION

Using #9 needles 18 sts x 24 rows = 4in (10cm) square.

ABBREVIATIONS

Pb (place bead) = bring yarn to front of work, bring bead up yarn to needle, push bead up tight to the needle, slip the next stitch purlwise, take yarn to back of work, knit 1.
Note: the method explaining beading on page 44 will place the bead in between the stitches. The method explained above is suitable for larger beads that sit on top of the stitch to give it a bobble effect.
K2tog (knit two stitches together)
P2tog (purl two stitches together)

METHOD

Knit in a combination of moss stitch and stockinette stitch.

Cast on 34 sts.

Row 1: K1, P1 to end.

Row 2: P1, K1 to end. (These 2 rows form moss stitch.)

Row 3: K2, *Pb, K1*, rep from * to * until last 2 sts, K2.

Row 4: Purl. (These last 2 rows form stockinette stitch.)

Row 5: K3, *Pb, K1*, rep from * to * until last st, K1.

Row 6: Purl.

Repeat last 6 rows until work measures 10½in (26.5cm).

Decreasing

1. K2tog. *K1, P1*, rep from * to * until last 2 sts, K2tog (32sts).

2. K2tog. *K1, P1*, rep from * to * until last 2 sts, K2tog (30sts).

3. K2tog. *Pb, K1*, rep from * to * until last 2 sts, K2tog (28sts).

4. P2tog. Purl to last 2 sts, P2tog (26sts).

5. K2tog. K1, *Pb, K1*, rep from * to * last 3 sts, K1, K2tog (24sts).

6. P2tog. Purl to last 2 sts, P2tog (22sts).

7. K2tog. *K1, P1*, rep from * to * until last 2 sts, K2tog (20sts).

8. K2tog. *K1, P1*, rep from * to * until last 2 sts, K2tog (18 sts).

9. K2tog. K2, *Pb, K1*, rep from * to * until last 2 sts, K2tog (16sts).

10. P2tog. Purl to last 2 sts, P2tog (14sts).

11. K2tog, K1, *Pb, K1*, rep from * to * until last 3 sts, K1, K2tog (12 sts).

12. P2tog. Purl to last 2 sts, P2tog (10sts).

13. K2tog. *K1, P1*, rep from * to * until last 2 sts, K2tog (8 sts).

14. K2tog. *K1, P1*, rep from * to * until last 2 sts, K2tog (6 sts).

15. Cast off.

Sew in ends.

Block and press.

Making up

1. Lay the knitted piece flat and measure a piece of lining ⅓in (1cm) bigger than the knitted piece to allow for the seam. Lay the front face of the lining to the front face of

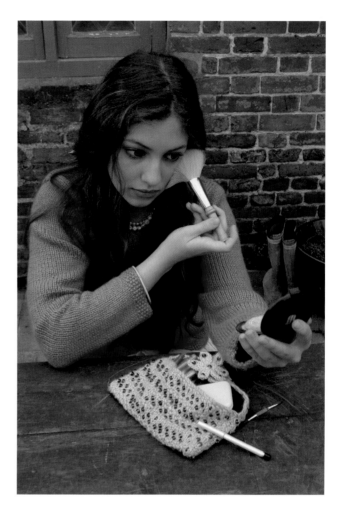

the knitted piece and machine-sew leaving one side of one of the decreased edges open. When stitching, leave the edges of the knitted stitches free, so the sides can be sewn up later.

2. Turn the fabric inside out to reveal the right side of the knitted piece. At the open edge, tuck the lining under and hand-stitch the rest of the lining to the knitted piece.

3. Fold so that the right sides are facing and bring the bottom edge of the fabric up to ⅛in (1cm) below the point where decreasing starts and stitch the two side seams using the over-and-over method (see page 40).

4. Gently press the seams. Sew a snap fastener on the inside of the flap. Sew beads on to each side petal of the knitted flower and attach to the front of the bag flap.

Funky cushions

Both of these cushions have been knitted to show off the beautiful colors of this Colinette yarn. The Silkychic yarn used in Cushion 1 is so soft, silky and sumptuous, it feels as if you are knitting with feathers. The combination of Firecracker and Point Five yarn used in Cushion 2 simply sparkles with light and color. The Firecracker yarn is just like satin to the touch and has an inviting fluffy texture.

CUSHION 1

EQUIPMENT

1 pair #8 needles

1 x 16in (40cm) cushion pad

Four large buttons

YARN

2 x 100g skeins Colinette Silkychic, shade Gaugin

TENSION

Using #8 needles 18 sts x 24 rows = 4in (10cm) square.

METHOD

Knit both panels in the same way, as follows:

Cast on 65 sts with #8 needles and knit in garter stitch (knit every row) until work measures 16in (40cm).

Cast off.

Making up

1. Sew in ends.
2. Join knitted sections along 3 seams.
3. Turn inside out.
4. Put the cushion pad into the cover and stitch across the top to secure.
5. Attach buttons to decorate.

Make 4 pom-poms (see page 45), and attach them by sewing one pom-pom into each corner of the cushion.

CUSHION 2

Panel 2

EQUIPMENT
1 pair #15 needles
1 pair #17 needles

YARN
2 x 100g skeins Colinette Firecracker, shade Turquoise
1 x 100g skein Colinette Point Five, shade Paint Box

TENSION
Using #15 needles with Firecracker yarn 8 sts x 12 rows =
4in (10cm) square.
Using #17 needles with Point Five yarn 7 sts x 9 rows = 4in
(10cm) square.

METHOD
Panel 1:

Cast on 40 sts with Firecracker yarn and #15 needles and
knit in stockinette stitch throughout (knit one row, purl one
row alternately).
Knit until work measures 16in (40cm).
Cast off.

Panel 2:

Cast on 35 sts with Point Five yarn and #17 needles and
knit in stockinette stitch throughout (knit one row, purl one
row alternately).
Knit until work measures 16in (40cm).
Cast off.

Making up

1. Sew in ends.
2. With right sides of the pieces facing, sew up 3 sides of
   the cushion.
3. Turn inside out.
4. Place the cushion pad inside the knitted pieces and
   stitch across the top to secure.
5. Thread a tape needle or a sewing needle with a large-
   enough eye to thread the Firecracker yarn.

Make 4 tassels (see page 46), and attach one to each
corner of the cushion securely.

 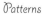

Button handbag

Once you've made this pretty button bag, others will be begging you to make more, so either pretend you bought it in a designer store, or buy plenty of yarn and be prepared to knit for your friends and family for the next year. The most fun aspect about making this bag is rummaging in junk stores for the prettiest buttons. Any yarn can be used and it can be knitted to any size – just use the size needles that are recommended for the yarn.

EQUIPMENT
1 pair #7 needles
Lining
1 snap fastener or Velcro fastening
80–100 buttons
Ribbon, 1¹/₂in (4cm) wide, 60in (1.5m) long

YARN
2 x 50g balls Rowan 4-ply Cotton, shade 129 Aegean (used in double thickness throughout)

TENSION
Using #7 needles 18 sts x 25 rows = 4in (10cm) square.

METHOD
Cast on 45 sts.

Rows 1–40: Work in stockinette stitch until work measures approx. 6in (15.25cm) .
Rows 41–42: *K1, P1* repeat *to* to end of row. This sets moss stitch.
Rows 43–63: Continue in moss stitch for a further 20 rows until the moss stitch rows measure approx. 3¹/₂in (9cm).
Rows 64–104: Work in stockinette stitch until total work measures approx. 15in (38.5cm) .
Cast off.

Making up
Sew in ends.
Block and press.

Lining
1. Lay the knitted piece flat and measure a piece of lining fabric ¹/₃in (1cm) bigger than the knitted piece to allow for the seam. Lay the front face of the fabric to the front face of the knitted piece and machine-sew 3 sides, leaving the top seam open. When stitching, leave the edges of the knitted stitches free so the sides can be sewn up later.
2. Turn the fabric inside out to reveal the right side of the knitted piece. Fold in half with wrong side facing.
3. Stitch up the side seams of the bag, stitching the knitted pieces together.
4. Turn the top seam under by 1in (2.5cm) and stitch.
5. Turn each end of ribbon under by ³/₄in (2cm) and stitch 4 sides of the ribbon to inside the side seams at the top of the bag.

Finishing
1. Sew the buttons randomly on the front of the bag, sewing through the lining to secure the buttons in place.
2. Sew the snap fastener or Velcro fastening to the inside of the bag.
3. Tie the ribbon in a bow and sew the bow in place to secure the strap.

Dog jackets

Well, of course they get cold – especially the little cute ones with hardly any fur. One glance in a dog-walking zone tells you that dog jackets are now all the rage and no pooch should be seen without one. Purely for fashion's sake substitute a cotton yarn for this Merino one for an alternative jacket – then your canine companion can look stylish in both the summer and winter months.

EQUIPMENT
1 pair #6 needles
1 pair #7 needles
1 set of 4 x #7 double-pointed needles

YARN
Shark coat:
Yarn A: Debbie Bliss Merino DK, shade 104
2 x 50g balls (for small size), 2 x 50g balls (for medium size),
3 x 50g balls (for large size)
Yarn B: 1 x 50g ball Debbie Bliss Merino DK, shade 101

Pom-pom coat:
Debbie Bliss Merino DK, shade 301
2 x 50g balls (for small size), 2 x 50g balls (for medium size),
3 x 50g balls (for large size)
Color oddments (for pom-poms)

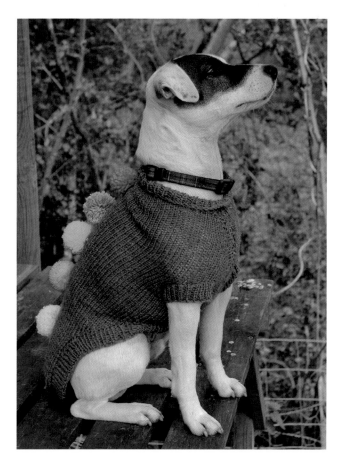

TENSION
Using #6 needles 22 sts x 28 rows = 4in (10cm) square.
Using #7 needles 20 sts x 26 rows = 4in (10cm) square.

METHOD
The instructions are written for the small size. If changes are necessary for medium or larger sizes, the instructions are given in brackets.

For the shark coat

Neck ribbing:

Cast on 47 [61/85] sts with yarn A and #6 needles.

Row 1: (Rs) K1 *P1, K1, rep from * to end.

Row 2: P1 *K1, P1, rep from * to end.

Repeat these two rows K1, P1, ribbing for a further 18 [20/22] rows ending on the 2nd row and increase 1 st in the middle of the last row, leaving you with 48 [62/86] sts. Break off yarn.

Change to #7 needles and proceed in stockinette stitch. You will need 2 separate balls of shade 101 (yarn B), so wind off half to split the ball in 2.

Row 1: Using yarn B, K3 [K6/K8], rejoin yarn A making sure you twist both colors to avoid a gap. Knit until the last 3 [6/8] sts. With the 2nd ball of yarn B, join yarn, twisting yarn A to avoid a gap, and K3 [K6/K8] sts in yarn B.

Row 2: Using yarn B, P3 [P6/P8]. Change to yarn A and purl until the last 3 [6/8] sts.
P3 [6/8] sts in yarn B.

Rows 3–7: Increase 1 st at each end of this and every following 4 rows, increasing your sts in yarn B and keeping 42 [50/78] sts between each end in yarn A, leaving you with 58 [72/104] sts.

Continue in stockinette stitch, increasing 1 st at each end of following knit row and every alternate row until you have 68 [82/122] sts.
P1 row.

Leg openings:

Both leg sections are worked at the same time, using separate balls of yarn for each section.

Row 1: Rs facing, use yarn B K7 [10/12], cast off 6 [6/10] sts. In yarn A, K42 [50/78] (including stitch on needle after cast off).
In yarn B, cast off 6 [6/10] sts. Knit until the end of row.

Row 2: Beginning with a purl row, work 9 rows in stockinette stitch from cast off sts, ending with Rs facing for next row.

Joining row:

Knit 7 [10/12] sts, turn and cast on 6 [6/10] sts, turn, K42 [50/78] sts, turn, cast on 6 [6/10] sts, turn, knit to end of row, leaving you with 68 [82/122] sts.

Continue until work after neck ribbing measures 9in [10/11½in] (23cm [25.5/29cm]) ending with a purl row. Place a marker at each end of last row.

Back shaping:

Rs facing, cast off 9 sts at beginning of next 2 rows, leaving you with 54 [64/96] sts.

Next row: K2tog, K until last 2 sts, K2tog.

Next row: Purl.

Repeat the last 2 rows until there are 36 [42/66] sts on needle (these will be yarn A).

Continue until work measures approx. 12½in [15½/21in] (32cm [39/53cm]) (or length required to base of tail) ending on a purl row.

Leave remaining 36 [42/66] sts on a stitch holder.

Sew neck seam to markers.

Back ribbing:

With Rs facing and double-pointed needles using yarn A and yarn B yarn where necessary, pick up and knit on first needle 40 [56/72] sts along body from marker to back, on 2nd needle.

K36 [42/66] sts from spare needle. On 3rd needle pick up and knit 40 [56/72] sts along opposite side of body to marker 116 [154/210] sts.

Place marker on 1st st. Work 8 rounds of K1, P1 ribbing. Cast off loosely in rib.

Leg ribbing:

Stitches to be picked up around the leg opening.

With first double-pointed needle, pick up and knit 10 [12/14] sts around the leg opening. With 2nd double-pointed needle, pick up and knit 10 [12/14] sts, and with 3rd needle pick up and knit 10 [12/14] sts, leaving a total of 30 [36/42] sts.

Place marker on the first st. Work 10 rounds of K1, P1 ribbing. Cast off very loosely in rib. This is the ribbing for the dog's legs and will be too tight if you cast off tightly.

Repeat for 2nd leg opening.

To make fin:
Using #7 needles and yarn A, cast on 3 sts.

Row 1: K1 yfwd K2 [4 sts].
Row 2 and every alternate row: Knit.
Row 3: K1 yfwd, K3 [5 sts].
Row 5: K1 yfwd, K4 [6 sts].
Row 7: K1 yfwd, K5 [7 sts].
Row 9: K1 yfwd, K6 [8 sts].
Row 11: K1 yfwd, K7 [9 sts].
Row 13: K1 yfwd, K8 [10 sts].

Row 15: K1 yfwd, K9 [11 sts].
Row 17: K1 yfwd, K10 [12 sts].
Row 19: K1 yfwd, K11 [13 sts].
Row 21: K yfwd, K12 [14 sts].
Row 22: Cast off 14 sts.

These 22 rows form the pattern.

For the pom-pom coat
Make as for the shark coat, but using one color throughout.

Making up
Make 2 and sew them together.
Shark coat: Sew the fin on the appropriate place on the back of the dog coat.
Pom-pom coat: Make 5 small pom-poms (see page 45) and attach along the back of the coat.

Rose top

The fashionably close fit of this wide-ribbed tank top is given a nostalgic, feminine touch by the delicate crochet trim. Be experimental and knit another version with the crochet in a contrast color or texture such as a silky thread. The top was originally intended to have a "bootlace" ribbon threaded through it, but the roses caught my eye in a local fabric store and seemed exactly right in form and color. Why not make your own ribbon collection and rethread them to suit your mood?

EQUIPMENT
1 pair #3 needles
Stitch holder
Row counter (optional)
Ribbon or braid, 1yd (1m) to thread as shown, 2yds (2m) if you want a bow at center front.

YARN
Debbie Bliss Baby Cashmerino, shade 503 Pea Green

SIZES
Small sizes are given in the instructions with medium, large and Xlarge in brackets. This sizing is based on a gentle stretch to the knitting that opens the ribs out but is not a skin-tight fit. As the main fabric is so stretchy, this is only a rough guide to the finished size – the best method is to knit a large tension swatch and see what stretch you prefer before choosing the size to knit.

	SMALL 6–8	MEDIUM 10–12	LARGE 14–16	XLARGE 16–18
Bust:	32–34in	36–38in	40–42½in	43–45in)
	(81–86cm)	(91–97cm)	(102–108cm)	(110–115cm
Finished bust:	34in	37in	41in	45in
	(86cm)	(94cm)	(104cm)	(112cm)
Finished length:	18½in	19in	20in	21in
	(46cm)	(48cm)	(50cm)	(52cm)

YARN
(number of 50g balls)

SMALL 6–8	MEDIUM 10–12	LARGE 14–16	XLARGE 16–18
9	11	13	15

TENSION
Using #3 needles with stockinette stitch 25 sts x 34 rows = 4in (10cm) square.

METHOD
When you come to sew up this garment, you will need to turn both pieces back to front – so what was the right side when knitting becomes the inside. This makes knitting the holes easier, while also positioning lace holes at the center front in a purl rib for a prettier threading of the ribbon.

Back
Cast on 108 [116/132/140] sts.

The main pattern, worked throughout:
Small and XL sizes:
*P4, K4, rep from * to last 4 sts, P4.
*K4, P4, rep from * to last 4 sts, K4. Rep these 2 rows.
M and L sizes:
*K4, P4, rep from * to last 4 sts, K4. Rep these 2 rows.
*P4, K4, rep from * to last 4 sts, P4.

Work 96 [97/97/86] rows in the main pattern until work measures 11in [11½/12½in] (28.5cm [29/29.5/30cm]) from cast on.

Underarm shaping:
Next row: Cast off 2 [2/3/8] sts at beginning of next 2 [2/2/2] rows.
Next row: Cast off 3 [3/2/1] sts at beginning of next 2 [2/2/2] rows.

Next row: Cast off 2 [2/3/1] sts at beginning of next 2 [2/2/2] rows.

Work 12 [14/12/12] rows, decreasing 1st at each end every 2 [2/2/2] rows.

Work 33 [37/47/49] rows straight.

Next row: Put in the lace holes across the middle 5 [5/5/5] knit stitch ribs. Working the lace holes on the knit stitch ribs is a simpler technique. Over the 4 sts on a "right" side row this is worked as *yf, K2tog, K2tog into back of stitch, yrn*. Work 3 rows straight.

Next row: Make 2 lace holes in each of the first knit ribs that are outside the middle 5 [5/5/5] knit stitch ribs.

Shoulder and neck shaping:

Next row: Cast off 4 [4/5/4] sts on the outer edge at beginning of row and work 37 [36/40/43] sts main pattern. Place remaining sts on a stitch holder.

Next row: Turn work and cast off 8 [8/9/10] sts at the neck edge, K to end.

Next row: Cast off 4 [4/5/4] sts on the outer edge, knit to end.

Next row: Cast off 4 [4/5/3] sts at the neck edge and make 1 lace hole in the neck edge end of the next knit stitch rib out towards the edge, knit to end.

Next row: Cast off 4 [5/5/4] sts on the outer edge and knit to end.

Next row: Cast off 4 [5/5/4] sts at the neck edge and knit to end.

Next row: Work 4 rows casting off 4 [5/5/4] sts on the outer edge every other row.

Next row: Cast off remaining sts.

Opposite side shoulder and neck shaping:

Row 1: Return held stitches to needle and cast off the middle 9 [9/11/11] sts, knit main pattern to end.

Next row: Work 1 row.

Next row: Turn work and cast off 8 [8/9/10] sts at the neck edge, K to end of row.

Next row: Cast off 4 [4/5/4] sts on the outer edge, knit to end.

Next row: Cast off 4 [4/5/3] sts at the neck edge and make

1 lace hole in the neck edge end of the next knit stitch rib out towards the edge, knit to end.

Next row: Cast off 4 [5/5/4] sts on the outer edge and knit to end.

Next row: Cast off 4 [5/5/4] sts at the neck edge and knit to end.

Next row: Work 4 rows casting off 4 [5/5/4] sts on the outer edge every other row.

Next row: Cast off remaining sts.

Front

Work as back to row 117 [123/127/131] or until work measures 14in [15/15/15$^{1}/_{2}$in] (35cm [37/38/39cm]) from cast-on edge.

Next row: Make lace holes across the middle 5 [5/5/5] knit ribs.

Next row: Work 3 rows.

Next row: Work 1 row, making 1 lace hole (yf, K2tog) at the central side of one knit stitch rib preceding and following the center 5.
Next row: Work 1 row.

Neck shaping:
Next row: Knit 33 [36/40/42] sts and place remaining stitches on a stitch holder.
Next row: Cast off 2 [2/2/3] sts at beginning (neck end) of row, K to end.
Next row: Work 1 row, making a lace hole (K2tog into back, yrn) in the outer end of the same knit stitch rib out from the center 5 (this "pairs" the hole made 4 rows earlier).
Next row: Work 5 [5/5/5] rows, casting off 2 [2/2/2] sts at beginning (neck end) of the first and every 2 [2/2/2] rows.
Next row: Work 1 row, making 1 lace hole (yf, K2tog) in the end nearest the neck of the next knit stitch rib out from the last one.
Next row: Work 2 [2/2/2] rows, casting off 1 [2/2/2] sts every 2 [2/2/2] rows.
Next row: Work 4 [4/4/4] rows, decreasing 1 [1/1/1] st every 2 [2/4/1] rows.
Next row: Work 1 row, making a lace hole (K2tog into back, yrn) in the outer end of the same knit stitch rib out from the last one (this "pairs" the hole made 4 rows earlier).
Next row: Work 5 [5/5/5] rows, decreasing 1 [1/1/1] st at the neck edge every 3 [2/4/2] rows.
Next row: Work 1 row, making a lace hole (K2tog into back, yrn) directly above the last hole.
Next row: Work 2 [2/2/2] rows, decreasing 1st every 2 [2/2/2] rows.
Next row: Work 5 rows straight.
Next row: Work 1 row, making a lace hole (K2tog into back, yrn) directly above the last hole.
Next row: Work 2 [6/8/10] rows straight.

Shoulder shaping:
Next row: Cast off 4 [4/5/4] sts at shoulder edge, K to end.
Next row: Work 4 [4/4/4] rows casting off 4 [5/5/4] sts at shoulder edge every other row.
Next row: Cast off 4 sts at shoulder edge, making a lace hole

(K2tog into back, yrn) directly above the last hole.
Next row: Work 4 [4/4/4] rows, casting off 4 [4/5/5] sts at shoulder edge every other row.
Next row: Work 1 row.
Next row: Cast off remaining sts.

Opposite neck and shoulder shaping:
Row 1: Return remaining sts back on to needle, cast off the center 16 sts and knit to end.
Next row: Work 1 row.
Next row: Cast off 2 [2/2/3] sts at beginning (neck end) of row, K to end.
Next row: Work 1 row, making a lace hole (K2tog into back, yrn) in the outer end of the same knit stitch rib out from the center 5 (this "pairs" the hole made 4 rows earlier).
Next row: Work 5 [5/5/5] rows, casting off 2 [2/2/2] sts at beginning (neck end) of 1st and every 2 [2/2/2] rows.
Next row: Work 1 row, making 1 lace hole (yf, K2tog) in the end nearest the neck of the next knit stitch rib out from the last one.
Next row: Work 2 [2/2/2] rows, casting off 1 [2/2/2] st every 2 [2/2/2] rows.
Next row: Work 4 [4/4/4] rows, decreasing 1 [1/1/1] st every 2 [2/4/1] rows.
Next row: Work 1 row, making a lace hole (K2tog into back, yrn) in the outer end of the same knit stitch rib out from the last one (this "pairs" the hole made 4 rows earlier).
Next row: Work 5 [5/5/5] rows, decreasing 1 [1/1/1] st at the neck edge every 3 [2/4/2] rows.
Next row: Work 1 row, making a lace hole (K2tog into back, yrn) directly above the last hole.
Next row: Work 2 [2/2/2] rows, decreasing 1st every 2 [2/2/2] rows.
Next row: Work 5 rows straight.
Next row: Work 1 row, making a lace hole (K2tog into back, yrn) directly above the last hole.
Next row: Work 2 [6/8/10] rows straight.

Shoulder shaping:
Next row: Cast off 4 [4/5/4] sts at shoulder edge, K to end.
Next row: Work 4 [4/4/4] rows casting off 4 [5/5/4] sts at shoulder edge every other row.

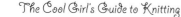The Cool Girl's Guide to Knitting

Next row: Cast off 4 sts at shoulder edge, making a lace hole (K2tog into back, yrn) directly above the last hole.

Next row: Work 4 [4/4/4] rows, casting off 4 [4/5/5] sts at shoulder edge every other row.

Next row: Work 1 row.

Next row: Cast off remaining sts.

Sleeves

These are the same for all sizes.

Sew shoulder seams with mattress stitch, matching ribs carefully. Note: Do not steam this garment if it is knitted in the specified yarn as the rib looses its elasticity when steamed.

Count up from the underarm on the armhole edge, and put a marker 10 rows up from the end of the shaping on both front and back. To make the pick-up even, mark your armhole again halfway between this marker and the shoulder seam. This gives you 4 equal sections to divide your stitches between.

Evenly pick up 44 [52/52/60] sts along the complete edge from front to back. (Numbers may vary with your personal knitting tension, but as a rough guide based on my tension, picking up 5 sts across 7 rows will give this result.)

Knit the main pattern across these sts, casting off 4 sts on alternate rows until there are 3 ribs left on the needles, Knit 1 row, then cast these off.

Making up

1. Sew the completed garment pieces together underarm with mattress stitch.

2. Crochet a basic crochet stitch completely around the sleeve edges and neck edge. Do not stretch the edge, but neither should you pull it tight.

3. Next, crochet a 6-chain loop along the edge of the base crochet, catching the chain into the edge every 3rd crochet stitch so the loops are forced out into a scallop effect.

4. Sew in the ends and thread a ribbon of your choice through the lace holes.

Yarn tote bag

This bag has been made using a cheap woollen blanket from a charity store that has been dyed bright pink with a washing-machine dye. It gives a really convincing impression of a hand-felted bag. Make sure you buy a blanket that is 100 percent natural fiber as the dye doesn't work on synthetic fibers. The hotter you wash it, the more felted it looks. If you make it up with smaller dimensions, it also makes a really hip handbag.

EQUIPMENT

1 blanket
1 pack of machine-dye (shown in Deep Pink)
Lining fabric
Sewing thread
Sewing-machine or hand-sewing needle
Pins
T-shirt transfer
12in (30.5cm) piece of light cotton, slightly larger than the image
Computer, scanner, and color printer
Iron

METHOD

1. Cut a piece of fabric 16 x 31in (40.5 x 79cm) for the bag and 2 pieces of fabric $4^1/_2$ x 25in (11.5 x 63.5cm) for the straps.
2. Cut a piece of lining the same size as the main piece of fabric.
3. Stitch the wrong side of the lining to the wrong side of the main fabric, so you have one piece of fabric.
4. Fold the fabric in half inside out, so the fold forms the bottom of the bag and it measures 16 x $15^1/_2$in (40.5 x 39.5cm).
5. Stitch up the sides using, leaving a $^5/_8$in (1.5cm) seam (1).

6. While the bag is still inside out, turn the top edge over $^1/_4$in (0.5cm) and press. Fold again another 1in (2.5cm) and stitch $^5/_8$in (1.5cm) from the fold (2). If you are using a blanket or a thick fabric, you may need to hand-stitch these seams.
7. To make the bag square at the bottom, keep the bag inside out, fold the side seam against the bottom seam, and stitch a 4in (10cm) line at the bottom of the triangle (3). The bag should now look like it has two little ears.
8. To make the handles, fold the 2 smaller pieces of fabric lengthwise right side facing. Sew a seam along the longest edge and one of the short ends, leaving one of the seams open. Turn the right side out (it is useful to use a knitting needle to poke the fabric through gently). Stitch the other seam (4).
9. Attach the handles $2^1/_2$in (6cm) in from each side seam. Stitch a rectangle to secure the handles (5).
10. Turn the bag right side out.

Image transfer

1. Find an image from your computer with which to decorate the bag.
2. Download and print on to a T-shirt transfer. Make sure you print with a mirror image for any text you want to print.
3. Iron the image on to a light piece of cotton, cut and stitch to neaten the edges, and stitch in place on to the front of the bag using a zig-zag or decorative stitch.
4. Leave the top end open and use as a pocket for scissors, tape, stitch holders, sewing-up needle or cell phone.

selvage

15½in (39.5cm)

16in (40.5cm)   4½in (1.5cm)

fold material

1.

2.   ¼in (0.5cm)

1in (2.5cm)   ⅝in (1.5cm)

3.

4.

5.

Needle Udder

It is so easy to lose your needles, so why not try making this simple needle case to carry around your most commonly used needles so you can always find the size you need?

EQUIPMENT

Cow fur fabric
Pink lining fabric
Tailor's chalk
Pink and black thread and sewing needles
Snap fastener
5 daisy buttons
20in (0.5m) cotton-covered elastic rope

METHOD

1. Cut a piece of lining 20 x 50in (51 x 127cm) (1).
2. Measure 28in (71cm) from one of the short edges, making a line with tailor's chalk. Fold the fabric from one short edge to this line, making a 14in (35.5cm) fold (2).
3. With tailor's chalk mark a line 8in (20.4cm) from the fold across the fabric. Starting at the 8in (20.4cm) line, mark a semi-circle towards the center of the fold (3).
4. Sew the arch of the semi-circle (4).
5. Trim the excess off corners (5).
6. Turn right side out and press.
7. At the opposite short edge, sew a 1in (2.5cm) hem (6).

8. From the bottom of the 1in (2.5cm) hem, fold the fabric 12in (30.5cm) (7).
9. Sew the side (long) edges from the bottom end to the beginning of the semi-circle (flap) (8).
10. Sew straight lines of varying widths to form about 10 needle pockets (9).
11. Cut a piece of fur fabric 15 x 22in (38cm x 56cm). Lay the lining on the wrong side of the fur. Turn the fur 1in (2.5cm) over the 3 straight sides of the lining to form a neat edge (10). Sew in place (11).
12. Turn the fabric over. Secure the flap to the fur by sewing a straight line along the final raw edge, taking care not to stitch the needle pockets closed (12).
13. Secure the fastner to the flap and to the corresponding opposite on the needle pockets. Sew a button on top of the flap to decorate and hide the snap fastener thread.
15. Cut the elastic rope into 2 equal pieces.
16. Thread 2 daisy buttons on to one of the elastic pieces and sew the ends of elastic together.
17. Sew one of these buttons to one edge of the roll, wrap the elastic round the roll and secure by looping the second button over first.
18. Repeat with the other 2 buttons and elastic for the other side.

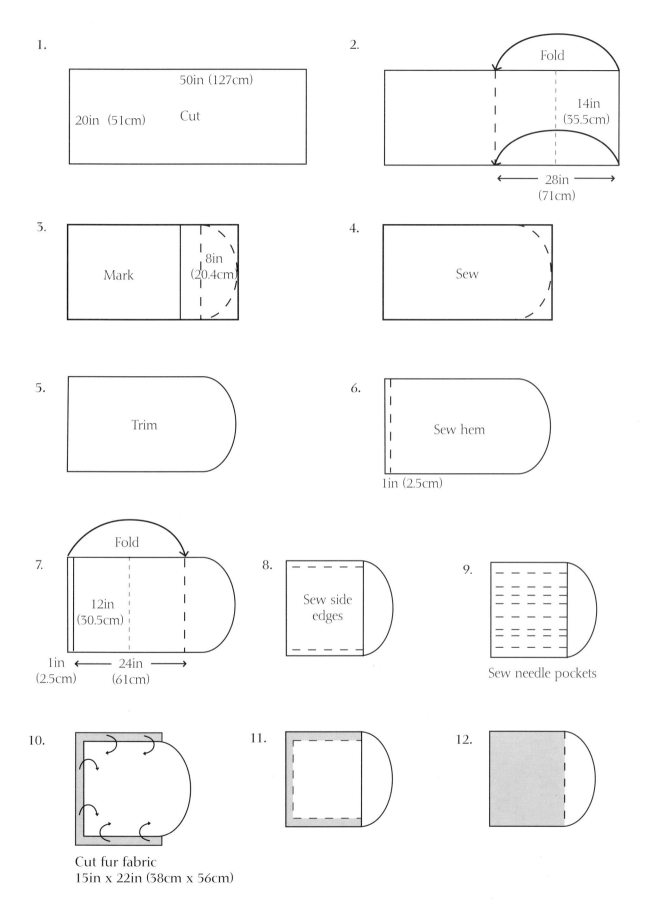

1. 50in (127cm)
   20in (51cm)   Cut

2. Fold
   14in (35.5cm)
   28in (71cm)

3. Mark   8in (20.4cm)

4. Sew

5. Trim

6. Sew hem
   1in (2.5cm)

7. Fold
   12in (30.5cm)
   1in (2.5cm)   24in (61cm)

8. Sew side edges

9. Sew needle pockets

10. Cut fur fabric
    15in x 22in (38cm x 56cm)

11.

12.

20 mistakes that every knitter should make

1   Knit one sleeve longer than the other.

2. You must drop a stitch so that it runs the whole way down your garment, which inevitably starts to unravel.

3. Knit the neck so tight that you can't get it over your head.

4. Knit the neck so loose that it shows your cleavage.

5. Knit something so itchy that it is never worn or means your boyfriend won't give you a hug because you're too itchy – a real passion killer.

6. Knit something fabulous and never sew it up, Throw it in the attic and don't see it for 20 years, by which time it'll be moth-eaten and home to refugee rats with a family of 56 aunts and uncles.

7. Don't count your stitches, so that instead of having straight lines your scarf looks like hourglasses stitched together.

8. Offer to knit a new boyfriend a woolly sweater – then he'll be scared off and will run a mile, because of too much commitment on your part.

9. Try to adapt something your knitting experience isn't ready for. Always follow the instructions, they are there to help.

10. Sew the wrong side to the right side. So you have the inside sleeve attached to the outside back.

11. Start knitting something for somebody's baby, take 18 years and give it to them just as they are about to leave home for college.

12. Wash your garment and then promptly shrink it after spending 10 years making it.

13. Knit a sweater for a relative as a gift without measuring them – Uncle Charlie always wanted a knitted dress.

14. Knit your partner a reindeer or snowman sweater for Christmas.

15. Let your cat sleep on your lap while knitting, then when it gets up find cat dribble all over your cashmere masterpiece.

16. Knit Fairisle and get the pattern totally muddled up so your garment looks like a sea of mangled color or Joseph's technicolor raincoat.

17. Go to Knit Nights every Monday and undo your knitting more than you actually knit.

18. Knit your stitches so tight that you can't get them off the needle.

19. Knit a bikini and swim in it. (Knitting swimming trunks is definitely not a mistake – it'll give you a laugh.)

20. Show your mother your knitting. She'll be of the old school of 1970s and 1980s feminists and will think you've let the team down.

Suppliers

USA

Knitting Fever Inc
35 Debevoise Avenue
Roosevelt, NY 11575
www.knittingfever.com

The Knitting Garden
25 Longmeadow Road
Uxbridge, MA 01569
www.theknittinggarden.com
email: Elizabeth@theknittinggarden.com
Tel: 888 381 9276

Purl
137 Sullivan Street
New York, NY 10012
Tel: 212 420 8796
www.store.purlsoho.com
email: customerservice@purlsoho.com

UK

Beads Unlimited
PO Box 1
Hove
Sussex BN3 3SG
www.beadsunlimited.co.uk
email: mailbox@beadsunlimited.co.uk
Tel: 01273 740777

Debbie Bliss
www.debbieblissonline.com
email: jane@designeryarns.uk.com

Colinette Yarns Ltd
Banwy Workshops
Llanfair Caereinion
Powys, Wales SY21 0SG
www.colinette.com
email: info@colinette.com
Tel: 01938 810128

Designer Yarns Ltd
Units 8-10 Newbridge Industrial Estate
Pitt Street
Keighley
West Yorkshire BD21 4PQ
www.designeryarns.uk.com
email: jane@designeryarns.uk.com
Tel: 01535 664222

Injabulo Buttons
(hand-made ceramic buttons)
Broom Cottage
Ashton
Oundle
Peterborough PE8 5LD
01832 274881
www.injabulo.com
Email: info@injabulo.com

John Lewis
For a list of stores visit:
www.johnlewis.com

Laughing Hens
PO Box 176
St Leonards on Sea
East Sussex TN38 0GZ
www.laughinghens.com
email: info@laughinghens.com
Tel: 01424 202010

Rowan Yarns
Green Lane Mill
Holmfirth
West Yorkshire HD9 2DX
www.knitrowan.co.uk
email: info@knitrowan.co.uk
Tel: 01484 681881

Useful addresses and other interesting knitting places

The Crafts Council (UK)
44a Pentonville Road
Islington
London
N1 9BY
020 7278 7700
www.craftscouncil.org.uk

Knit Café
8441 Melrose Avenue
Los Angeles, CA 90069
Tel: 323 658 5648
www.knitcafe.com
email: knitcafe@aol.com

Knitting & Crochet Guild (UK)
PO Box HH1
Leeds
LS8 2YB
www.knitting-and-crochet-guild.
org.uk

The Knitting Guild of America
PO Box 3388
Zanesville, OH 43702-3388
www.tkga.com
email Tkga@tkga.com

Vogue Knitting
www.vogueknitting.com

Cast Off (UK)
London
www.castoff.info
email: info@castoff.info

Extreme Knitters
www.xtremeknitting.com

Knitty Magazine
http://www.knitty.com/
ISSUEwinter04/index.html

Knitting software resources:
http://knitting.about.com/
library/weekly/aa071397.htm

**Try this knitting quiz to
test your knowledge:**

http://www.funtrivia.com/
playquiz.cfm?qid=6151&origin

Index